C000273539

T
STEPMOTHER

by Githa Sowerby

SAMUEL FRENCH

FOR AMATEUR PRODUCTION ENQUIRIES

UNITED KINGDOM AND WORLD
EXCLUDING NORTH AMERICA
licensing@concordtheatricals.co.uk
020-7054-7298

Each title is subject to availability from Concord Theatricals,
depending upon country of performance.

---

written permission of the publisher. No one shall share this title, or part of this title, to any social media or file hosting websites.

The moral right of Githa Sowerby to be identified as author of this work has been asserted in accordance with Section 77 of the Copyright, Designs and Patents Act 1988.

USE OF COPYRIGHTED MUSIC

A licence issued by Concord Theatricals to perform this play does not include permission to use the incidental music specified in this publication. In the United Kingdom: Where the place of performance is already licensed by the PERFORMING RIGHT SOCIETY (PRS) a return of the music used must be made to them. If the place of performance is not so licensed then application should be made to PRS for Music (www.prsformusic.com). A separate and additional licence from PHONOGRAPHIC PERFORMANCE LTD (www.ppluk.com) may be needed whenever commercial recordings are used. Outside the United Kingdom: Please contact the appropriate music licensing authority in your territory for the rights to any incidental music.

USE OF COPYRIGHTED THIRD-PARTY MATERIALS

Licensees are solely responsible for obtaining formal written permission from copyright owners to use copyrighted third-party materials (e.g., artworks, logos) in the performance of this play and are strongly cautioned to do so. If no such permission is obtained by the licensee, then the licensee must use only original materials that the licensee owns and controls. Licensees are solely responsible and liable for clearances of all third-party copyrighted materials, and shall indemnify the copyright owners of the play(s) and their licensing agent, Concord Theatricals Ltd., against any costs, expenses, losses and liabilities arising from the use of such copyrighted third-party materials by licensees.

IMPORTANT BILLING AND CREDIT REQUIREMENTS

If you have obtained performance rights to this title, please refer to your licensing agreement for important billing and credit requirements.

**Other plays by GITHA SOWERBY
published by Samuel French**

A Man and Some Women

Before Breakfast

Direct Action

Rutherford and Son

Sheila

The Policeman's Whistle

**FIND PERFECT PLAYS TO PERFORM AT
www.samuelfrench.co.uk/perform**

ABOUT THE AUTHOR

Katherine Githa Sowerby was born in 1876 in Gateshead, England. Her first play, *Rutherford & Son*, was an outstanding success when originally performed in 1912. Published under her initials G.K. Sowerby, it was generally assumed that the author was a man. When her true identity was revealed she became an overnight sensation. *Rutherford & Son* ran for one hundred and thirty-three performances in London and sixty-three performances in New York and was translated into numerous languages. Other plays followed: *Before Breakfast*, 1912; *A Man and Some Women*, 1914; *Sheila*, in 1917; *The Stepmother*, 1924; and finally, *The Policeman's Whistle*, 1934. She was well-known in the early twentieth century as a feminist and voice of the people, but she by the time of her death in 1970, she and her works had lapsed into obscurity.

Rutherford & Son was revived in 1980 and there have been numerous productions since. Samuel French are publishing *The Stepmother* to coincide with the 2017 production at the Chichester Theatre.

CHARACTERS

CHARLOTTE GAYDON

MARY

EUSTACE GAYDON

MONICA
BETTY } His daughters

MR BENNET

MISS LOIS RELPH

CYRIL BENNET

PETER HOLLAND

MRS GEDDES

SCENES

PROLOGUE

A sitting room in **EUSTACE GAYDON**'s *house at Chilworth.*

There are big windows centre at back, fireplace right and the doors are up left leading into the hall and down right leading to the rest of the house. The room has an old-fashioned look without being ugly. There is a big writing table centre. It is late on a winter afternoon.

CHARLOTTE GAYDON *is sitting, knitting in an armchair by the fire. She is about sixty years of age, with a mild face already old. She carries herself with that gently deprecating air which in her generation seems to have been considered suitable to the lady who failed to justify her existence by marriage. All her life has been devoted to filling the gaps left by other people and the fact that she has never had any business of her own in the world has smoothed down any individual characteristics she might have had to a dead level of adaptability.*

MARY *comes in from the hall. She is carrying a lighted lamp which she puts on the table beside* **CHARLOTTE**.

CHARLOTTE *(mildly reproving)* You're late, Mary. I've been waiting.

MARY I'm sorry, miss. It's got dark soon tonight.

CHARLOTTE Perhaps I had better have my lamp at five in future, instead of half-past.

MARY *(turning up the lamp)* Very well, miss. It'll be nice when we have the electric light. *(She goes to the windows to draw the curtains)*

CHARLOTTE Electric light?

MARY Mr Gaydon was saying this morning that he was going to have it put in one of these days.

CHARLOTTE *(after a moment)* That will be nice, Mary.

MARY Yes, miss. Most of the big houses in Chilworth have had it this long time. *(She comes back to make up the fire)* Miss Turner's sent home your dress.

CHARLOTTE *(interested)* Oh! Does it look right?

MARY The crêpe's deeper than it was in the pattern.

CHARLOTTE I wanted it deep. I like mourning to look like mourning.

MARY *(doubtfully)* Yes, miss.

CHARLOTTE Do you mean there's something wrong with it, Mary?

MARY Well, it seems to me she's made it look more like a widow than an aunt.

CHARLOTTE *(with gentle dignity)* I'll see about it presently. You might make up the fire while you're here.

MARY *(who has already done so)* Yes, miss. *(She puts the fire irons back in their places – on her way to the door she stops)* Shall I lay dinner for two, or three?

There is a slight pause.

CHARLOTTE For two, Mary. *(She goes on with her knitting)*

MARY *(tentatively)* I thought perhaps Miss Relph might be dining with you and Mr Gaydon.

CHARLOTTE No.

MARY Very good, miss. *(She still lingers)* She always dined with Mrs Brent, the parlourmaid told me.

CHARLOTTE As my poor niece's companion, she naturally would do so. *(She looks up uneasily)* I did ask Mr Gaydon about her having her meals with us, but he seemed to think it would be unsuitable.

MARY I'll lay for two then.

CHARLOTTE If you please.

MARY goes to the door.

Mary!

MARY Yes, miss?

CHARLOTTE There will be no harm in your talking a little to Miss Relph when you take up her dinner, if she seems lonely.

MARY Yes, miss.

She opens the door and meets **EUSTACE** *coming in.*

I beg your pardon, sir.

EUSTACE Any letters, Mary?

MARY No, sir.

EUSTACE The post's come?

MARY Yes, sir – there was only one for the servants' hall.

EUSTACE GAYDON *is a thin, spare man of forty-five with a jerky manner and a ready laugh. His eyes are keen and as restless as a bird's. There is a touch of the dandy in his dress – just enough to give an extra suggestion of prosperity and well-being. A pleasant, shrewd, rather charming man, with just that something genuine about him wanting – warmth, humanity, whatever your name for it may be – which leaves you wondering why you don't quite like him. The voices of both women have brightened as he comes in.*

CHARLOTTE *(smiling at him)* Will you have tea, dear?

EUSTACE Please, Mary.

MARY goes out.

(He warms his hands at the fire) It's queer there's nothing from Bennet.

CHARLOTTE *(surprised)* Mr Bennet? Are you expecting to hear from him?

EUSTACE Yes – I wrote to him. As a matter of fact I wanted to settle this question of Fanny's will.

CHARLOTTE I thought you'd decided she hadn't left one.

EUSTACE Well, I've searched the house, and there isn't anything at the bank—

CHARLOTTE And surely, dear, she would never have gone to Mr Bennet.

EUSTACE Why shouldn't she?

CHARLOTTE When she knew you'd quarrelled with him?

EUSTACE I'm afraid I can't flatter myself that my opinion carried much weight with Fanny... Besides, I didn't quarrel with Bennet – I simply ceased to employ him as my solicitor.

CHARLOTTE I meant that, dear... What happens if there is no will?

EUSTACE Everything comes to me. That's why I think there is one.

CHARLOTTE *(sighing)* Oh, Eustace!

EUSTACE It's no use blinking matters, Aunt Charlotte. Fanny didn't like me.

CHARLOTTE *(quickly)* She misjudged you.

EUSTACE Perhaps. But the result's the same. What she has probably done is to leave it over my head to my children.

CHARLOTTE If she has – I shall never be able to feel the same about her again – never!

EUSTACE Oh, well. Everybody doesn't think of me as you do, Aunt Charlotte.

CHARLOTTE Everybody doesn't know you as I do.

EUSTACE Fanny had her queer side like the rest of us. And her chief foible was to manage her own affairs in her own way.

CHARLOTTE I can't understand that. A widow alone in the world – with a brother like you ready to take it all off her shoulders – I'm sure I never had a moment's peace till I put everything into your hands.

MARY *comes in with tea.* CHARLOTTE *goes to the table to pour it out.* MARY *goes out.*

EUSTACE *(casually)* I suppose you didn't ever mention to Fanny that you had done that?

CHARLOTTE *(her mind on the tea)* Done what, dear?

EUSTACE Handed your affairs over to me.

CHARLOTTE Of course not – you told me not to.

EUSTACE Did I? Well, I don't think you'll regret it. Though I sometimes wonder if I ought to have let you do it.

CHARLOTTE *(tranquilly, pouring out tea)* My dear Eustace!

EUSTACE That's all very well, but it's a big responsibility for me. Of course, as long as you're content to make your home in my house and take your allowance of pin-money—

CHARLOTTE What more could I ask? *(She hands him his cup)*

EUSTACE *(chaffing her)* Well, I acknowledge the advantage isn't all on my side, eh? You're a brick, Aunt Charlotte – I can say anything to you.

CHARLOTTE *(flattered)* Can you?

EUSTACE Anything. For instance – for the last six months or so haven't you just now and then had a doubt of me at the back of your mind?

CHARLOTTE Doubt of you? Eustace!

EUSTACE I don't mean of me personally. But of – well, the way things were going with me?

CHARLOTTE *(timidly)* Of course, dear, I've guessed that you were – a little short of money. The housekeeping books—

EUSTACE I thought so. Well, I'll tell you now it's over. I've been a bit hard up.

CHARLOTTE But why, dear? How can you be hard up?

EUSTACE One thing and another. Delays. Certain things that ought to have gone well have been hanging fire—

CHARLOTTE *(anxiously)* But it's going to be all right?

EUSTACE Bless you, yes, as right as rain. Everybody has their ups and downs – and I'm glad to say that my financial position at the present time is as sound as it ever was.

CHARLOTTE *(simply)* How much do you suppose Fanny has left?

EUSTACE *(as if she had changed the subject)* Fanny? It's difficult to say. She ought to have had...let me see – twenty-five or thirty thousand – but I'm not counting on that. Though it's queer that Bennet hasn't written...if she has a will.

CHARLOTTE It's a lot of money. I remember once Fanny saying to me—

MONICA *and* BETTY *appear at the door, piloted by* MARY. *They are pretty children of seven and nine and have evidently had their hair tidied and their spirits suppressed for the ceremony of saying goodnight.*

(Her eyes on the children) Years ago, just at the time you broke with Mr Bennet... *(Changing into the spiritless sing-song which some grown-ups still feel the right tone for children)* Well, dears – have you come to say goodnight to Father and Aunt Charlotte?

EUSTACE *(absently)* Bedtime for little girls?

MONICA *(the elder)* Goodnight, Father.

BETTY Goodnight, Father.

EUSTACE *(kissing them mechanically)* Been good children, eh? That's right.

CHARLOTTE Come and say goodnight quietly – Father and Aunt Charlotte are busy.

They cross to her obediently. She is fond of them both, but hugging and kissing of children being outside her scheme of up-bringing, she offers her cheek.

MONICA *(bursting with the news)* Miss Relph's got a silver box on her dressing table.

CHARLOTTE Has she, dear – that's right.

BETTY And a brush with a silver back – Aunt Fanny gave them to her on her birthday.

MONICA Two birthdays, Betty.

BETTY No, it wasn't, it was both together.

MONICA Do people give two birthday presents for the same birthday, Aunt Charlotte?

CHARLOTTE Never mind, we'll talk about it tomorrow. Go to nurse quietly now, like good children.

They go, breaking into a run as they reach the door.

MONICA *(as they disappear)* It was two.

EUSTACE What was it you were saying?

CHARLOTTE Was I saying something?

EUSTACE About Fanny. And Bennet.

CHARLOTTE *(vaguely)* Oh, yes. It was only that she asked me why you had parted with him – when he and his father had been the family solicitors for so long.

EUSTACE Well – you told her, I suppose?

CHARLOTTE I couldn't, dear, I didn't know.

EUSTACE I hope you didn't lead Fanny to suppose there was anything wrong – anything on his part, I mean?

CHARLOTTE *(getting up to close the door which the children had left open)* Oh, no! She had too much faith in him to think that.

EUSTACE *(his manner more jerky than usual)* Bennet's old-fashioned – slow – too slow for me by a long way. Every scheme I put to him was full of dangers and difficulties. I got tired of being held up at last, and I left him, that was all. We're civil enough now – when we meet.

CHARLOTTE *(whose attention has wandered)* Eustace, what are you going to do about Miss Relph?

EUSTACE *(busy with his own thoughts)* I don't know. Why?

CHARLOTTE Something will have to be arranged for her, I suppose.

EUSTACE Plenty of time for that. She's all right as she is for the present. *(He takes up The Times and sits in the armchair beside the fire)*

CHARLOTTE Oh, quite – so long as you don't mind her being here.

EUSTACE Well, to tell the truth, I don't altogether like it.

CHARLOTTE *(standing behind his chair, her hand on the back of it)* I'm sorry, dear – but she seemed so frightened and nervous. She...she was with Fanny when she died. I just felt I couldn't leave her alone in that empty house with no one but the caretaker—

EUSTACE That's all right. I only meant I don't want her to imagine she is going to be provided for indefinitely.

CHARLOTTE Oh, there's no fear of that. She quite understands that she will have to find another situation. I've been thinking. How would it be if she stayed on here for a time... as governess?

EUSTACE Oh, I don't think that would be a good plan.

CHARLOTTE She speaks French. And she's good at making clothes she tells me.

EUSTACE You wouldn't think it, to look at her... No, it's too much like making oneself responsible for her. Giving her a home and all that. After all, she's not my business – poor girl. What is it?

CHARLOTTE *(who has been listening)* I thought I heard a bell.

EUSTACE I didn't. *(He listens a moment, then goes on)* I don't mind giving her a bit to go on with – a month's salary, whatever it was Fanny gave her. And that reminds me, you'd like a cheque.

CHARLOTTE Oh, thank you, dear. Yes. *(He gets up and goes to the writing table, centre)*

EUSTACE Will a hundred see you through for a bit?

CHARLOTTE I'm afraid not, dear.

EUSTACE Why – how much are you behindhand?

CHARLOTTE There are so many outstanding bills—

EUSTACE Well, a hundred and fifty?

CHARLOTTE Yes, that would do for the present.

EUSTACE *(taking his chequebook)* Sorry to have held you up, old lady. It won't happen again.

CHARLOTTE You're always so nice about everything, Eustace. I hate worrying you.

He writes. After a moment **MARY** *comes in, closing the door after her and stands waiting.*

EUSTACE *(without looking up)* Well, Mary?

MARY A gentleman to see you, sir. *(She hands him a card)*

There is a pause.

CHARLOTTE Who is it, dear?

EUSTACE Bennet...

CHARLOTTE Mary! You haven't left him standing in the hall?

MARY He won't come in, miss. He's just called to ask Mr Gaydon for an address.

Another pause.

EUSTACE *(getting up)* You'd better go, Aunt Charlotte, if you don't mind.

CHARLOTTE Oh, yes, dear, certainly – Mary...

They gather up her knitting bag and various stray balls of wool. **CHARLOTTE** *flutters out by the door down right,* **MARY** *following.* **EUSTACE** *goes to the other door and flings it open.*

EUSTACE That you, Bennet? Don't stand out there in the cold. Come in here, will you?

He comes back immediately so that **BENNET** *is more or less obliged to follow him.*

BENNET *(resenting this)* I told your servant I wouldn't keep you a minute.

EUSTACE That's all right. Sit down, won't you?

BENNET I won't, thanks. I hadn't intended to call but it occurred to me on my way home that it might shorten matters if I did. You aren't on the telephone?

EUSTACE No. I'm always meaning to have it put in... You got my letter?

BENNET *(looks at him)* Haven't you had mine?

EUSTACE No.

BENNET Oh, then – you don't know.

EUSTACE There is a will then?

BENNET *(slowly)* Oh, yes, there's a will...not a very satisfactory one for you, I'm afraid.

EUSTACE Oh? When was it made?

BENNET In nineteen-six. Soon after Miss Relph went to live with your sister.

EUSTACE What has Miss Relph to do with it?

BENNET That depends on whether she was living with your sister at the time of her death.

EUSTACE Supposing she was?

BENNET She gets everything.

There is a silence.

I'm sorry to put it so bluntly, but – well – there it is, I'm afraid. *(He fills up another pause by taking a notebook out of his pocket)*

EUSTACE There it is... Who's executor?

BENNET I am.

EUSTACE And trustee, I suppose?

BENNET There is no trust.

EUSTACE There's no one in it except you and Miss Relph?

BENNET No one. *(His tone indicates that* EUSTACE *is going a little too far)* In justice to Mrs Brent—

EUSTACE Justice! Thirty thousand pounds to a girl who would have been handsomely dealt with in a legacy with the other servants. If that's your idea of justice—

BENNET I didn't say it was. It isn't a lawyer's business to criticise his clients.

EUSTACE Or to prevent them making fools of themselves.

BENNET Look here, Gaydon, I'm ready to make allowances for you being disappointed—

EUSTACE I'm not disappointed.

BENNET In that case I'm not ready to make allowances.

EUSTACE Come, come, Bennet – I'm sorry if I seem abrupt...
When I say I'm not disappointed, I mean for myself. I
expected nothing and I've got nothing. But – well, I think
you might have put in a word for my children.

BENNET I can't discuss that. My business was to carry out your
sister's instructions—

EUSTACE You had influence with her.

BENNET None whatever. Nor I believe had anyone else.

EUSTACE Except Miss Relph!

BENNET I don't know anything about Miss Relph.

EUSTACE Nobody does. You know how reserved my sister was,
always making mysteries out of nothing – not a word could
I get out of her beyond that she'd known the girl's mother
– picked her up in some hotel abroad – and that she'd died
suddenly, leaving this child penniless. And here she is, with
thirty thousand pounds to her name—

BENNET *(pulling him up)* Can you give me her address. *(Pause)*

EUSTACE This is her address.

BENNET She's here? In your house?

EUSTACE Yes, my aunt brought her here this morning.

BENNET In that case – could I see her?

EUSTACE What – now?

BENNET If you have no objection.

Pause.

EUSTACE Look here, Bennet, as man to man – is there no way
of getting round this will?

BENNET *(who has known this was coming)* No, there isn't.

EUSTACE How about undue influence?

BENNET There's no suggestion of such a thing.

EUSTACE Ah... *(He stands thinking intently)*

> **BENNET** *takes out his watch with an impatient movement.*

BENNET I really must be off. If Miss Relph could spare me a few minutes before I go...

EUSTACE I'm afraid she can't see you tonight.

BENNET Why not?

EUSTACE She's ill.

BENNET Ill?

EUSTACE So my aunt says. My sister's death has been a great shock to her... I really shouldn't like to run the risk of upsetting her – more than she is upset already. *(A silence)* If you care to come and see her here, in a few days, when she's fit again, do by all means.

BENNET *(slowly)* Thanks... I'll write to her.

EUSTACE Just as you please.

> **BENNET** *moves to go.*

How's the boy?

BENNET *(in the same tone)* Cyril? He's very fit, thanks.

EUSTACE Getting on, isn't he? How old is he now?

BENNET *(at the door)* Sixteen. Don't trouble – I'll let myself out. Goodnight.

EUSTACE Goodnight.

> **BENNET** *goes out.*

EUSTACE stands where he is – half-way to the door – till the front door bangs. Then his face slowly changes. He makes a furious movement.

(under his breath) Damn you, Fanny! Damn you!

Presently his eyes wander to the writing table. He goes to it, picks up the cheque he had written and tears it up; stands thinking hard. Then crosses to the bell and rings. He stands motionless till **MARY** *comes in.*

Where's Miss Relph?

MARY In her room, sir.

EUSTACE Ask her to come and speak to me for a moment.

MARY Yes, sir.

She goes got.

After a time the door re-opens to admit **MISS RELPH**: *a straight little black-clad figure. Her dress and the plain fashion in which she wears her hair do nothing to help her beauty; her face is colourless and her eyes have a wide, strained look. It is difficult to imagine what she would be like if she were happy and natural. She has the look of youth overweighted by association with middle-age; and her manner is between that of a servant and a child who has never played with other children.* **EUSTACE** *bows to her. She makes an awkward movement in return.*

EUSTACE Good evening.

MISS RELPH Good evening.

EUSTACE I thought it might be as well if you and I had a little talk.

MISS RELPH Thank you, Mr Gaydon.

EUSTACE Sit down, won't you?

*She follows his movement to a chair beside the writing
table and sits facing the audience with her hands on
her lap. He comes to the chair behind the table.*

(with a movement of his pipe) You don't mind my smoking?

MISS RELPH *(unaccustomed to this kind of courtesy)* No, thank
you.

He sits. There is a silence.

EUSTACE Will you forgive me if I ask an impertinent question?

MISS RELPH I – anything you would like to ask, Mr Gaydon—

EUSTACE How old are you?

MISS RELPH Nineteen.

EUSTACE That makes you fourteen when you went to live in
my sister's house... What was your position there?

MISS RELPH My position?

EUSTACE She had some sort of arrangement with you, I presume.

MISS RELPH There was no arrangement.

EUSTACE You simply lived with her as companion or secretary
or whatever it was...with some sort of a salary, of course—

MISS RELPH I had no salary.

Slight pause.

EUSTACE But, my dear Miss Relph, do you really mean to tell
me that my sister accepted your services without payment
of any kind?

MISS RELPH *(looks at him)* Oh, no – I didn't mean that! She –
gave me things. Everything I had in the world came from her.

EUSTACE I see... It didn't occur to you that that was rather to
my sister's advantage?

MISS RELPH Oh, you don't understand – Mrs Brent was good
to me – she—

EUSTACE In a sense she was. You were an orphan and penniless, and she took you into her house and fed and clothed you. That was one side of the bargain. Being a business man I see another. I don't want to say anything that may seem like criticism of my sister now she's gone, but... I think she might have thought of you a little.

MISS RELPH She was very kind to me.

EUSTACE I mean, as to your future.

MISS RELPH Oh, that was all settled.

He looks quickly at her.

EUSTACE But you tell me there was no arrangement between you.

MISS RELPH No arrangement about money. *(A pause)*

EUSTACE *(coldly)* Perhaps you would prefer not to discuss this, Miss Relph?

MISS RELPH *(distressed)* Oh, no – it's only too kind of you to—

EUSTACE *(with growing feeling)* Of course, if you'd rather keep things to yourself—

MISS RELPH Oh, please, Mr Gaydon—

EUSTACE Then won't you tell me in what way my sister had provided for your future?

MISS RELPH *(eagerly)* I was to live with her.

EUSTACE But afterwards? When she wasn't there for you to live with?

MISS RELPH She never spoke of that. We were to go on just as we were for always.

EUSTACE *(slowly)* And the end of it is that you find yourself cut adrift, without money or a home. *(She makes no reply)* That is so...isn't it?

MISS RELPH Yes.

EUSTACE *(his voice deliberately grave and kind)* I'm sorry for you, Miss Relph.

MISS RELPH Sorry – for me?

EUSTACE I think you have been hardly dealt with – I pity you very much.

This is too much for her, she covers her face with her hands. Her crying is as sudden as a child's, and like everything about her, awkward and restrained.

(who has achieved his object more suddenly than he expected) My dear Miss Relph, you mustn't give way like this. There's nothing to cry about.

She cries afresh.

Things are bad, I admit, but crying won't mend them... This is very distressing for me.

MISS RELPH I'm very sorry.

EUSTACE Come, come! Tell me what's the matter... Is it something I've said?

MISS RELPH No!

EUSTACE Then what is it? *(He waits)* I'm only trying to help you, you know.

MISS RELPH *(shivering)* I'm frightened.

EUSTACE Frightened – what's there to be frightened of?

MISS RELPH Oh, you don't know what it's been like – alone in that empty house.

EUSTACE But I do know – that's why I had you brought here.

MISS RELPH There was a bell in my room for her to ring at night when she couldn't sleep. Every night since she died, I've lain and watched it, waiting for it to ring. Once I thought it began to move – just a little to and fro—

EUSTACE My dear girl, this is nonsense!

MISS RELPH I saw it – I did.

EUSTACE Bells don't ring unless there's someone there to ring them.

MISS RELPH In the daytime when I went into her room and saw her, I knew she was dead, but... I've been with her so long night and day, I couldn't believe but that she would want me and – somehow – come for me.

EUSTACE Stop that – do you hear? Stop it!

She straightens herself up.

You're overdone – you've got things on your nerves. Dry your eyes. Put your handkerchief away.

Now, listen to me. That's all over – do you understand? There's nothing to frighten you in my house – no bells or bogies or any nonsense of that kind. I don't allow them.

MRS RELPH I'm sorry...to be so idi-otic.

EUSTACE You're a baby. And my pipe's out.

He gets up and goes to the fireplace for a match. While his back is turned she gets her handkerchief out, quickly wipes away the remains of her tears and puts it away again.

(turning with his sudden smile) Feeling better?

MISS RELPH *(with a ghost of a smile answering his)* Yes, thank you.

EUSTACE That's right. Now – just a word more about your future and I won't worry you any more tonight. Have you made any plans?

MISS RELPH I'm afraid not.

EUSTACE Well, don't. Let the whole thing slide. Just stay on here with me. Just feel that this is your home and that I'm here to come to – a friend – whenever you want help or advice. How's that?

MISS RELPH You mean – to live here?

EUSTACE Why not?

MISS RELPH In your house?

EUSTACE *(smiling at her)* Till you're tired of us – of course.

MISS RELPH Oh, Mr Gaydon... I can't thank you. I can't say what I feel.

EUSTACE That's all right. I can't say what I feel either. But – well, I'm old-fashioned, and I hate the idea of a woman working, fighting for her living among strangers.

MISS RELPH But, Mr Gaydon...if I have no money – I must work.

EUSTACE Well, work for me then.

MISS RELPH Could I?

EUSTACE If you feel you must do something...teach the children... you speak French, don't you?

MISS RELPH Oh, yes, my mother was French. And I can make clothes.

EUSTACE Really? That thing you've got on now is very nice – did you make that?

MISS RELPH Oh, yes.

EUSTACE There you are then – teach those two young monkeys of mine and make their clothes. Have you seen them yet?

MISS RELPH Just for a moment – they came into my room. I'd really hardly talked to children before—

EUSTACE Hold out your hand.

She obeys, wondering; he puts some money into it.

MISS RELPH Oh, no – please, I can't take this—

EUSTACE Nonsense – I want you to.

MISS RELPH *(holding it out to him)* I can't take money I haven't earned.

EUSTACE *(takes her hand and closes it)* Just to please me.

There is a pause; they are silent.

MISS RELPH *(all her soul in her voice)* I'll work for it. I'll work for you. *(He lets go of her hand)*

EUSTACE There's one thing we're forgetting... A possibility.

MISS RELPH What?

EUSTACE We may find that my sister has left you something in her will.

MISS RELPH *(She shakes her head)* Me? Oh, no!

EUSTACE Why "oh, no!" Such things do happen?

MISS RELPH She would have told me.

EUSTACE It isn't likely certainly. But if she has...our little bargain's off, I suppose.

MISS RELPH Do you mean you wouldn't want me to stay?

EUSTACE I think you wouldn't want to stay.

MISS RELPH Oh, how can you think that? As if I could ever forget your goodness to me.

EUSTACE Ah, well – make no promises. I think you mean what you say. I hope you do... Now, run along. We shall be late for dinner. *(He ushers her to the door and opens it for her)* And remember...no more listening for bells, do you hear?

MISS RELPH Thank you, Mr Gaydon.

She goes out. He closes the door and walks over to the fireplace and rings the bell. Goes to the door – down right – opens it and stands waiting till MARY *comes in.*

MARY You rang, sir?

EUSTACE Miss Relph will dine with us.

MARY Tonight, sir?

EUSTACE For the future.

MARY Yes, sir.

Curtain.

ACT I

Scene I

The same, on a warm evening in September. Most of the old furniture remains, but re-arrangement has softened the formality of the room and the red curtains are no more. It looks pleasant and home-like as it never did under **CHARLOTTE***'s rule. It is lit now by the electric light* **MARY** *heralded ten years ago, but* **CHARLOTTE** *still sticks to her paraffin lamp; it is burning on the table beside her chair, like a flag still hoisted against the on-rush of modern conditions. She sits by the fire now – a gentle, rather querulous old lady with only a fitful interest in things going on around her. Everything has been done to make her old age soft and attractive and she wears a grey silk dress and a pretty lace cap. She is asleep at the moment and her face is peaceful.*

MONICA GAYDON *is sitting in an armchair, trying to fix her attention on a novel. At a table near her,* **BETTY** *is tying artificial flowers together. They are as unlike as sisters generally are.* **MONICA** *is extremely pretty. Her movements, perhaps because she has never played golf or hockey, and is young enough to have escaped the discipline of the war, are curiously gentle and noiseless. She has character and her own way of doing things. Nearly all of the few men she has met have made love to her, so that she has stepped straight out of the school room into a passive acceptance of her purely feminine destiny without the interval of struggle and self-consciousness which most girls go through. She is charmingly dressed in a dance frock of the simple-looking expensive kind.*

BETTY *is two years younger and still in her colt stage. She has only just put her hair up and wears her evening frock as if it were a tweed tailor-made. She is a type common enough in her generation – outspoken and entirely natural, with a healthy hardness and that curiously gawky attitude towards emotion which modern education seems to engender in girls – rather like what you see in a schoolboy towards his mother when she is saying goodbye on the station platform. She is pretty, or would be if she knew it, but so far, no man has told her anything more important about herself than that she is a jolly good sort and ought to play quite a decent game if she works at it.*

BETTY   I do wonder who'll be there?

MONICA   *(rather peevishly)* You've said that before, Betty.

BETTY   Well, I do wonder.

MONICA   Who should be there? Mrs Travers' dances are always the same.

BETTY   This isn't going to be. She's got eighteen men; strange ones, Connie told me so this morning.

MONICA   Some of them'll have to dance on the stairs then – or in the garden. *(Returns to her book)*

BETTY   I don't know why you're crabbing this dance. You've been doing it all day.

MONICA   I haven't – I only don't see why you're excited about it.

BETTY   I'm not excited, I'm anxious. It's all very well for you – you've got Cyril Bennet to dance with.

MONICA   Why don't you arrange beforehand like everyone else?

BETTY   There isn't anyone to arrange with.

MONICA   *(lazily)* Oh, nonsense.

BETTY   'Tisn't nonsense, it's the beastly truth. Look at me tonight. As likely as not I shall be sitting on the bank half the time.

MONICA You'll be all right.

BETTY *(putting down the flowers for a moment)* Do you ever feel shy?

MONICA Never – except with Cyril.

BETTY Men don't like me. *(She resumes her work)*

MONICA *(lazily)* What nonsense, Betty. Cyril loves you; and so does Peter.

BETTY They're different. Cyril belongs to you and Peter doesn't count – he's a friend of the family. Honestly, Monica – can you imagine anyone falling in love with me?

MONICA We're sisters, Betty.

BETTY Oh, dash! *(She throws down her scissors with a clatter)*

MONICA *(looking towards* CHARLOTTE*)* Sh – you'll wake her.

BETTY She's all right – she never hears anything now.

MONICA She will if you throw things about.

They wait a moment to see if she wakes.

BETTY I don't know why she's taken to sitting in here lately – we're always having to sh!

MONICA *(gently, still looking at* CHARLOTTE*)* It's because she doesn't like being alone, Mother says. *(In a different tone, restlessly)* I wish Mother would come.

BETTY She said she wouldn't be able to catch the early train.

MONICA She never does now. How much longer are you going to muddle with those flowers?

BETTY Till I get them right.

MONICA *(taking them from her)* Here, let me.

BETTY Why, you've got your ring on!

MONICA *(quietly)* Well?

BETTY Are you going to wear it?

MONICA I'm engaged to be married, and I'm going to wear my ring.

BETTY But it isn't settled.

MONICA It's going to be. I'm going to talk to Mother.

BETTY Why not talk to Father for a change?

MONICA What's the use? I tried to this afternoon. *(Gives the flowers to* **BETTY***)*

BETTY *(looking at the flowers in her hand)* I thought you'd had a row, by the way he chaffed you at dinner.

MONICA Oh, it's like hitting a pillow, trying to get anything out of Father. He won't do anything. And here he is going away tomorrow for weeks. *(She has gone to the window and opened it wide)*

BETTY I wish you hadn't to bother Mother, just at present.

MONICA Why at present?

BETTY Mother's worrying.

MONICA *(turning her head)* Worrying? Do you mean about money?

BETTY I don't know.

MONICA It can't be money, Ginevra's is doing so well – she said yesterday she had more orders for frocks than she could carry out.

BETTY It's Father probably.

MONICA Why should it be? I mean, he hasn't been any different from what he always is.

BETTY Mother's different. She calls it being cross.

MONICA Well, if she is, we don't mind having our noses bitten off – at least I don't, and anyway Cyril and I can't go on as we are any longer.

CHARLOTTE, *who has been slowly waking, begins to listen.*

BETTY *(getting up and going to try the effects of her flowers in a mirror up stage)* Oh, well – I'm glad Peter's come back, that's one thing.

MONICA I don't see what Peter's got to do with my engagement.

BETTY He's someone for Mother to make a pal of... I believe she missed him frightfully while he's been away. Look, Monica. How's that? *(The flowers)*

MONICA Rotten.

BETTY I knew you'd say that.

MONICA *(she sees that CHARLOTTE is awake and speaks more gently)* Hullo, Aunt Charlotte. I thought you were asleep.

She and BETTY, look at each other with an uncomfortable recollection of what they have been talking about.

CHARLOTTE What's Peter Holland come back for?

BETTY *(raising her voice slightly as they all do to CHARLOTTE)* Because the vacation's over, and the courts are sitting again.

CHARLOTTE When he went away, he said it was for a long time.

BETTY Well, so it is – it's three months.

CHARLOTTE Three months isn't a long time.

BETTY *(amused)* What do you mean, Aunt Charlotte?

CHARLOTTE Never mind what I mean. Where's your mother?

BETTY She's coming by the later train – *(mischievously)* and Peter's coming in to see her.

CHARLOTTE Tonight? A nice time to pay a call.

BETTY Peter doesn't pay calls, Aunt Charlotte, he pops in. That's the advantage of having his garden next to ours.

MONICA *(making a diversion)* Ssh, Betty. Have you seen my new frock, Aunt Charlotte?

CHARLOTTE You have too many frocks.

MONICA What's the use of having a fashionable dressmaker in the family if you don't have lots?

CHARLOTTE Dressmaker! They used to come in for three and sixpence a day and their dinner on a tray – and you talk as if it were a thing to be proud of.

BETTY *(taking up the cudgels)* We are proud of it, I'd like to know how many people could do what Mother's done?

CHARLOTTE I'm not talking about what she's done. I say that people are forgetting their dignity in these days – buying and selling like shopkeepers.

MONICA My dear Aunt Charlotte, if you only knew how frightfully old-fashioned we are compared with other people... That's Mother now. *(She goes to the door)*

BETTY Do you mean to say that a person who can earn money and make lovely things is to sit at home with her hands in front of her?

LOIS – *pronounced Lowis – comes in. She has changed considerably since the night we saw her. It is ten years since she became* **EUSTACE**'s *wife, housekeeper and governess. She is now twenty-nine, and like many women who have missed their girlhood and developed late, is physically and mentally at her best. She is well turned out in every detail. She has had a busy day and the practical side of her is still uppermost – but her way of speaking has the sound of strain, a trifle high-pitched and over-cheerful, that you hear in voices of women who are over-worked and whose business it is not to appear so.*

MONICA *(going to her)* Hullo, Mother darling.

LOIS Well, children, any news.

MONICA *(kissing her)* No. You're very late.

LOIS Yes, I had work to do and my train crawled.

CHARLOTTE *(peevishly)* Here you are at last.

LOIS *(going to her)* Hullo, Aunt Charlotte, I didn't see you tucked away there.

MONICA Have you had dinner.

LOIS *(kissing* CHARLOTTE*)* Yes, I had something with Mrs Geddes. *(To* BETTY*)* My dear child, what have you got there?

BETTY Where?

LOIS On your frock.

BETTY Flowers.

LOIS Please take them off. At once.

BETTY No Mother...

LOIS Yes, Mother. Who made that frock?

BETTY You did, of course.

LOIS Ginevra's did. And if you think Ginevra's is going to send you to a dance with one-and-elevenpence-worth of paper flowers on your dear little waist, you're mistaken.

BETTY They're not paper.

LOIS Calico then – don't argue with me when I come home in a bad temper.

CHARLOTTE There – just what I say. You're wearing yourself out with this business of yours.

LOIS Well, I make a profit on it, and if I am snappy, it's the family's contribution to put up with me. Ring the bell, Betty, there's a dear.

CHARLOTTE I don't know why you ever started it.

LOIS *(taking off her hat)* Don't you?

CHARLOTTE When I was young—

MONICA Mother's tired, Aunt Charlotte. And we've been through that once tonight.

LOIS Through what?

MONICA *(helping her)* Oh, all about ladies sitting at home and doing their housekeeping like when Aunt Charlotte was young.

CHARLOTTE A hobby's all very well. But when it takes you out of the house from morning till night, it can't be right.

LOIS Do you call Ginevra's a hobby, Aunt Charlotte?

CHARLOTTE Eustace says it is – and he ought to know.

LOIS *(quietly)* When did Eustace say that?

CHARLOTTE When? He jokes about it. "Never have a wife with a hobby" he says to people. And they laugh.

LOIS Eustace likes to make people laugh...

CHARLOTTE Oh, you're proud of yourself. I know that.

LOIS I'm proud of Ginevra's. I've made it.

CHARLOTTE And what's it doing for you? Rushing off in the morning, working all day, rushing back at night, tired out. You'll get to look old before you know where you are, and you won't like that.

LOIS I am old.

MONICA You, Mother!

BETTY *(indignantly)* What rot, Aunt Charlotte!

LOIS *(slowly)* It's my birthday tomorrow. If I were a German, how many candles do you think I'd have on my cake? Twenty-nine – there's a conflagration.

CHARLOTTE You will make fun.

LOIS Fun! I've been brooding over it all the way from town.

   MARY *has come into the room.* **LOIS** *breaks off.*

MARY You rang'm.

LOIS *(her voice dispirited)* Did I?... Oh yes, just to tell you I'd had dinner.

MARY Very good'm. Shall I take your things.

LOIS Please. I won't change. Any letters for me?

MARY They're on your table'm.

> **LOIS** *crosses to it,* **MARY** *takes up* **LOIS**'s *hat etc.*

CHARLOTTE My lamp, Mary.

MARY *(pausing)* Is there something wrong with it, miss?

CHARLOTTE I want it. Bring it, please.

> **MARY** *looks at* **LOIS** *who puts down a half-opened letter and comes quietly back to* **CHARLOTTE**.

LOIS Mary will bring it, dear – in a moment.

> *She makes a sign to* **MARY** *– who goes out – and half-kneels in front of* **CHARLOTTE**. *She speaks with a new gentleness.*

How have you been today?

CHARLOTTE *(looking into her face, answering her tone)* Very tired.

LOIS How's that?

CHARLOTTE I don't know. I've done nothing but sit here.

LOIS Didn't you go out in your chair?

CHARLOTTE No. There was no sun – I was tired.

BETTY *(who has not heard the incident of the lamp)* Why it's been a perfectly gorgeous day.

CHARLOTTE There was no sun.

BETTY But it's been cooking – don't you remember, Aunt Charlotte?

LOIS Betty... You'll go out tomorrow, I'll speak to Mary about it.

CHARLOTTE *(feebly gathering herself up, to* **BETTY***)* And I'll speak to you, Elizabeth. You're a very naughty, impertinent girl. *(Subsiding weakly into tears)*

BETTY *(startled by the tears)* I'm very sorry, Aunt Charlotte. I didn't mean to vex you.

LOIS You shouldn't contradict, Betty.

CHARLOTTE It's your fault – you let them talk to you as if you were their sister instead of their stepmother.

BETTY I've said I'm sorry.

CHARLOTTE I daresay – till next time – I'll go to my room. Perhaps I'll get a little peace there.

LOIS *(helping her to rise)* Yes, dear, do.

    CHARLOTTE*'s spectacles slip from her knee as she rises.*

CHARLOTTE I've dropped something.

LOIS Betty.

BETTY *(comes and picks them up, subdued)* Your spectacles, Aunt Charlotte.

CHARLOTTE *(looking at them)* My what?

BETTY *(louder)* Your spectacles... Aren't you well, Aunt Charlotte?

CHARLOTTE Well? Of course I'm well. What are you looking at me like that for?

LOIS Hasn't Aunt Charlotte just told you she's tired?

CHARLOTTE Of course I'm well.

BETTY *(in the same subdued, wondering tone)* Goodnight, Aunt Charlotte.

MONICA *(absorbed in her thoughts of her own affairs)* Goodnight.

CHARLOTTE Goodnight.

LOIS I'll come up later and read your chapter to you.

CHARLOTTE Oh, very well. But don't be long. Last night you were five minutes late.

LOIS Was I, I'm sorry dear.

CHARLOTTE —Leaving me to sit looking by the fire – with nothing to think about—

She goes out. **LOIS** *stands looking after her before she closes the doors.*

BETTY I'm sure there's something wrong with her. She's always forgetting things now.

LOIS Old people do forget things – poor darlings.

BETTY Poor you, I think. You do have a rotten time when you come home. If it isn't Aunt Charlotte it's us – and if it isn't us, it's—

LOIS Don't talk nonsense.

MONICA Go and tidy, Betty.

BETTY Presently.

MONICA It's nearly nine, and you're always late.

BETTY Mother – do you really mean I'm not to wear my flowers?

LOIS Your what?

MONICA Oh, don't grind on about your flowers, Betty – Mother's tired.

BETTY *(holding them against her frock)* I'm too white with nothing, I know I am. Do look, Mother.

LOIS *(with sudden irritation)* Mother, Mother – I wish you wouldn't call me that every other minute – I might be fifty to hear you.

BETTY *(rather taken aback)* Why, whatever else are we to call you?

LOIS *(repenting of her irritation)* Oh, I don't know – anything—
(She moves across to her writing table)

MONICA Peter says we ought to call you Lois – he was talking about it today.

BETTY As if we could, when we've called you Mother ever since you married Father.

LOIS *(her back to them)* Peter... Has Peter come back?

MONICA Oh, yes, I forgot to tell you. He turned up this morning, and he's coming to see you.

LOIS When?

MONICA Tonight.

BETTY I tell you what – I'll go and fasten them on properly and then you'll see what they really look like.

MONICA Yes, do – for goodness sake.

BETTY *goes out by door right.*

LOIS *moves slowly across to the fireplace and sits in* **CHARLOTTE**'s *chair.*

(standing in front of her) Mother, when am I going to be married?

LOIS My dear child! *(There is new life in her voice)*

MONICA No, I mean it. Something must be settled.

LOIS Of course, but—

MONICA Cyril and I have been talking. We've been engaged for a year and we're determined we're not going to hang on any longer.

LOIS But why scold me about it? You know I'm on your side.

MONICA Father isn't.

LOIS Have you spoken to him?

MONICA Yes – and we had a sort of a row about it. At least I had a row and he laughed.

LOIS Oh, my dear –

MONICA You know Father when you want to pin him down to anything... Cyril is talking to Mr Bennet to try to make him see Father before he sails tomorrow. I told him this – and he went on about my being too young and seeing about it when he comes back from America – till I could have hit him. And we ended off just when we began – *(passionately)* where we always end, where we'll end if we wait for another ten years. *(Pause)*

LOIS It hasn't been altogether his fault – Mr Bennet's been against it from the first. Cyril can't marry on his pay.

MONICA *(quickly)* He could, if I had something as well.

LOIS I see.

MONICA *(urging her)* Couldn't he, Mother?

LOIS Yes, of course... You must have a little patience, my dear. These things aren't settled in five minutes.

MONICA *(in a new tone)* Mother, why is Mr Bennet so against Cyril marrying me?

LOIS *(lightly)* Oh, Cyril's a bit of a catch, isn't he?

MONICA Oh, I know I'm not good enough. But there's something else... Something about Father.

LOIS *(quietly)* What do you mean?

MONICA I don't know.

LOIS You must know.

MONICA *(not looking at her)* He told Cyril that he wouldn't mind his marrying me if I weren't Eustace Gaydon's daughter. *(Pause)*

LOIS And you – interpret that, as something against Father?

MONICA What else could it be?

LOIS People say anything when they're angry – things that have no meaning. Mr Bennet used to be the family lawyer years ago and Father ceased to employ him. He probably resents that.

MONICA *(obstinately)* I want to know what Mr Bennet meant.

LOIS Well, you shall know. I'll ask him myself.

MONICA *(brightening)* Do you mean you'll see him? Oh, Mother, when?

LOIS When he gives me the opportunity.

MONICA Now you're talking like Father.

LOIS Oh, my dear child, you're both so young, surely you can wait just a little?

MONICA No, Mother – if you're going to talk about our age—

LOIS I'm talking about your youth.

MONICA I'm older than you were when you married.

LOIS That isn't the same thing.

MONICA Oh, everyone says that. *(Sharply)* I suppose if Cyril were about fifty, or whatever Father was, you'd think it was all right.

LOIS Monica!

MONICA *(passionately)* No one understands, not even you – *(seeing her face)* I'm sorry I said that, I didn't mean to say it – I only meant – it must have been different, you and Father.

LOIS It was different.

MONICA I don't know what's the matter with me. I'm always saying things I don't mean now, even to Cyril – it's the waiting – the wanting to be together, by ourselves – *(she is suddenly in tears)*

LOIS *(very gently)* When I said you were young, I didn't mean I wanted to put you off. I was thinking of all the years of happiness you've got in front of you – with nothing in the way.

MONICA I don't know what you call nothing.

LOIS You love each other – and you're free.

MONICA *(beginning again)* What's the good of that when we never get any further?

BETTY *comes in suddenly.*

Oh, what is it, Betty?

BETTY *(concentrated)* Father – matches.

MONICA *(irritated at the interruption)* There aren't any here, I gave the box to Cyril this morning.

BETTY *(drifting about the room)* Father wants matches. Help can't you?

MONICA What's the use of looking when there aren't any?

LOIS *(moving)* Ring for Mary. Or go and ask her for some.

BETTY Father has rung, he says, and no one answered.

EUSTACE *comes in, fussed and irritable, an unlighted pipe in his hand.*

EUSTACE *(bitterly)* None here, either I suppose.

LOIS Look on my table, Betty.

EUSTACE *(to MONICA)* Can't you do something?

MONICA *(turning away)* I have. I've rung for Mary.

EUSTACE Rung for Mary! You might as well ring for the dead.

BETTY Here are some.

EUSTACE Ah – hidden away, as usual, just where no one would look for them.

MARY *comes in.*

LOIS It's all right, Mary. Mr Gaydon has got what he wanted.

MARY Thank you'm.

She goes out, followed by BETTY.

EUSTACE *(lighting up on the hearthrug)* It's all very well, but it seems to me the servants are becoming uncommonly slack.

LOIS I'm afraid that's because I'm not here to look after them.

EUSTACE *(his irritation dying out as suddenly as it came)* You should make these girls do more. Here's one of them wanting to get married, and she knows as much about housekeeping as a baby. Eh?

No response from MONICA.

(jerking it out suddenly) I'm off tonight.

LOIS *(looks up)* Tonight? I thought you weren't going till the morning.

EUSTACE So I was, but I've got a man to see before I sail... *(A pause. Facetiously)* I suppose I can change my own mind if I like, eh?

MONICA *(dismayed)* But, Father, I told you Mr Bennet might want to see you tonight.

LOIS About that, Eustace. Monica wants something settled.

She takes up some knitting – a bright coloured silk thing, and settles down to it – she works quietly through the following scene.

EUSTACE *(pleasantly)* Monica and I have already discussed the subject.

MONICA I know, Father, but—

EUSTACE There's no but about it. I'm not going to be rushed into agreeing to things I haven't had time to think about.

MONICA Time! We've been—

EUSTACE Look here, my child – you spoke to me this afternoon in a way I'm not accustomed to – and not content with that, you worry and annoy your mother when she comes home tired.

MONICA There's no other time, she's always tired.

EUSTACE Don't answer me, please.

MONICA What else do you mean me to do?

EUSTACE To try and remember that there is someone else in the family to be considered besides yourself.

MONICA I do remember it...

LOIS *(quietly bringing them back to the point)* Cyril has seen his father today, Eustace. The idea was that you and he might meet and come to some arrangement.

EUSTACE Arrangement! What's there to arrange about?

MONICA *(catching at this)* Money, Father – what I'm to have. And giving your consent.

EUSTACE Money? What you're to have? My dear child – have you no self-respect – no dignity?

MONICA *(taken aback at the new tone)* Father!

EUSTACE You ask me to meet Cyril's father to bargain for the price he puts on marrying you – to bribe a man to marry my daughter—

MONICA *(indignantly)* Bribe! Cyril would marry me tomorrow.

EUSTACE Then why doesn't he? I'm not preventing him.

MONICA How can he, when we haven't enough to live on?

EUSTACE Exactly! That's my point, I take the old-fashioned view that a man must be prepared to support his wife in the style to which she has been accustomed.

MONICA Oh!

LOIS It isn't a question of bargaining or bribing – only of a settlement in the usual way.

EUSTACE It's like Bennet to begin talking of settlements.

LOIS He hasn't Eustace – he's never raised the question of money at all.

EUSTACE Then why are we discussing it?

LOIS So that you may have something definite to tell him when you see him.

EUSTACE *(laughs a little)* I think I see Bennet giving in gracefully – a greed grasping fellow if ever there was one.

LOIS If you think that he's behaving badly, why not tell him so?

MONICA He can't do that, Mother.

EUSTACE Surely Monica, this is for your mother and me to decide.

MONICA *restrains herself.*

I'm only waiting for a chance to give him a piece of my mind – as he knows very well.

LOIS But you may be away some time. It may mean waiting for weeks if you go tonight.

MONICA Yes, Father.

EUSTACE "Yes, Father" – I repeat that this is for your mother and me to decide.

MONICA *(losing patience)* Oh, decide then!

LOIS Monica—

MONICA I can't bear it, I can't. What's the use of trying to talk about it? You put me off this afternoon, joking and laughing at me, and I know well enough you're going away tonight on purpose. And when you come back it'll be just the same – till I'm never married at all – *(her little outburst ends in tears and—)*

She goes out.

EUSTACE *(laughing a little, tolerantly)* Well, upon my soul... that child wants a tonic or something.

LOIS What is your reason for not giving her a settlement?

EUSTACE Oh, good heavens, how you do grind on at a thing – haven't I said...

LOIS I don't mean what you say before Monica – I mean your real reason.

EUSTACE What I say before Monica is perfectly just and reasonable. *(Blustering)* If I can't fork out at a moment's notice, that isn't to say that something can't be arranged later. After the marriage instead of before...there's nothing so extraordinary about that, is there?

LOIS Mr Bennet won't consent to that.

EUSTACE I'm not going to put up with this stand and deliver attitude from Bennet or anyone.

LOIS *(putting down her work)* Do you mean – simply, that you can't give her a settlement?

EUSTACE I mean that it isn't convenient.

LOIS Oh, Eustace...

EUSTACE Now, for Heaven's sake don't begin to look as if the skies were falling because I tell you I'm a bit hard up. You make me feel I can't say the simplest thing without your jumping to the conclusion that things are ten times worse than they are.

LOIS But what are we going to do?

EUSTACE Talk to Bennet – you, I mean – make him think it's all right. Get them married...dash it, you're good enough at managing people when you want to – manage this.

LOIS Make him think it's all right? Isn't it all right?

EUSTACE Of course it is – haven't I just told you so.

LOIS Eustace – how bad are things?

EUSTACE Oh, you're beyond me altogether... If you must know – certain things that should have gone well are hanging fire – that's all.

LOIS You said that five years ago, when I started Ginevra's.

EUSTACE Well, we're five years nearer being all right. Good heavens! Didn't I set you up – even to buying the houses for you to set up shop in? How bad did you suppose things were when I was able to do that?

LOIS But you did that with my money, with part of what your sister left me.

EUSTACE What does it matter whose money it was? We're married people.

LOIS But the house isn't mine. It was bought in your name.

EUSTACE Oh, nonsense – the house is yours all right. Whatever has set you off talking about this tonight?

LOIS Because I'm always thinking about it. I know nothing – I don't even know what my own money's invested in.

EUSTACE My dear girl – how long do you suppose it would take to go into every investment I've made for you? Besides we're discussing Monica's marriage – do let us stick to the point.

LOIS If only you'd tell me how I stand. You don't know what it's like for me to go on working in the dark, spending everything I make, as I make it.

EUSTACE *(hardly)* Now we're getting to it.

LOIS *(pleadingly)* It's true, Eustace. How much have you given me for the last four years – ever since Ginevra's began to pay? A hundred pounds here, two hundred there – how far do you suppose that goes to running a house like this?

EUSTACE I've told you that's only temporary. Just go on for a bit longer as you are and you'll wake up one morning to find you're a rich woman.

LOIS Suppose I have a run of bad luck – suppose I fall ill. Oh, that's what wears me. If I fail, the whole thing fails.

EUSTACE You mustn't fail.

LOIS Mustn't – that's what I say to myself when I come home at night, too tired to sleep.

Pause. He looks uneasily at her.

EUSTACE You're feeling all right – aren't you?

LOIS *(almost laughs)* Oh!

EUSTACE It's all this worrying yourself about things that aren't going to happen... Why should you be ill? You never have been... Come, come, it's not like you to hunt bogies. Ginevra's is a flourishing concern – about as likely to have a bad year as the Bank of England.

LOIS It's as likely to have a bad year as any other business that depends on one person.

EUSTACE *(cheerfully)* Well – when that happens – come to me.

LOIS *(looks at him)* I have come to you.

EUSTACE When?

LOIS Now.

EUSTACE Oh, for Monica. That's a different thing.

LOIS There's nothing more important than that – there never could be – and you won't do it.

EUSTACE Cyril Bennet isn't the only man in the world.

LOIS *(with a sort of fear)* Eustace, this marriage is to happen – somehow. I've made up my mind to that.

EUSTACE *(easily)* It'll happen all right. All you've got do is to see Bennet. *(Looking at his watch)* What's the time? I must be off.

LOIS *(in a changed tone)* You leave it to me, then?

EUSTACE If you like – it doesn't matter which of us it is.

LOIS Then I shall act as I think best.

EUSTACE All right. Only for heaven's sake don't worry yourself ill about it. You're like all women – you don't know how to save yourself. *(He moves to go)*

LOIS Eustace!

EUSTACE Well?

LOIS *(slowly)* You say – that if ever I am in difficulties I can come to you.

EUSTACE Well, I mean it. But you won't be in difficulties.

LOIS That means – if I want a sum of money for any purpose I can rely on your being able to let me have it. I don't mean fifty pounds or a hundred. I mean my own money, the capital.

EUSTACE *(pulled up for a moment)* My dear girl, sensible people don't meddle with their capital.

LOIS Sensible people do, for a big purpose.

EUSTACE We needn't discuss that.

LOIS You will, then... Say you will.

EUSTACE *(impatiently)* Of course I will; but I assure you there isn't the slightest need to worry about the future. As for what you've spent on the house – I look on that as lent to me. *(Coming to her)* And a fine bill for arrears you'll be coming to me with some day – eh? Goodnight, I'm off.

LOIS When are you coming back?

EUSTACE Can't say. A few weeks, probably. Depends on how things go. *(He offers to kiss her – she puts her cheek up mechanically. Sarcastically)* Oh, thank you.

LOIS Oh, Eustace.

EUSTACE *(with a sort of dull anger)* You're an affectionate woman, Lois, upon my soul. *(She moves away)* I'll cable my address – in case you should feel up to sending me a line.

He goes out, injured. She stands by the fire, tired and dispirited.

MONICA *comes in by the door right.*

MONICA *(still under the influence of her tears)* Well?

LOIS Well, what?

MONICA He hasn't said anything, I suppose?

LOIS I think it will be all right. *(Pause)*

MONICA Do you mean to say you've actually got him to decide?

LOIS *(repeating wearily)* I think it will be all right.

MONICA Mother—

LOIS *(she takes out a cigarette)*... Oh – matches again... Make me a spill, there's a dear.

MONICA *(joyously)* Mother, you're a genius, an absolute genius. *(She tears a piece of paper)*

LOIS I said a spill, not half The Times.

MONICA Now we'll get a move on. Now I'm going to be happy – utterly and absolutely happy...

LOIS Without a regret?

MONICA *(holding out the lighted spill)* Regret? What's there to regret if we're going to be married?

LOIS Nothing, of course. Mind my nose!

MONICA *(sobered for the moment)* Do you mean – leaving you? I'm not going to leave you – it'll be just the same when I'm married.

A whistle is heard from the garden.

LOIS Everyone says that.

MONICA *(running to the window)* That's Cyril now... Come in, Cyril – it's all right – Father's gone.

CYRIL *enters. He is a good-looking, attractive young man with pleasant manners and something boyish about him that will probably last his lifetime.*

CYRIL Gone? *(Blankly)* Oh, I say... Good evening, Mrs Gaydon.

LOIS Good evening.

CYRIL I've just told the guvnor he's at home and he's coming along to see him now.

LOIS Now?

MONICA It's all right – Mother's going to see him instead – yes, you are, Mother.

LOIS I can't see Mr Bennet at a moment's notice. You must see I can't.

MONICA Oh, Mother dear, do.

LOIS I must have time to think.

CYRIL Please do, Mrs Gaydon – you don't know how difficult it's been to get him up to it.

LOIS *(giving in)* Oh, you two – very well, I'll see him. *(Going to door right)* But don't blame me if he walks out and slams the door.

MONICA Darling! Where are you going?

LOIS *(has gone to door right)* I can't face an angry parent, looking like a tramp. I'll get Betty to throw me into a frock.

MONICA Oh, all right. But do hurry.

LOIS *goes out.*

What did he say?

CYRIL Precious little. I did the talking.

MONICA What did you say?

CYRIL I said – I said – that I'd absolutely made up my mind to marry you; that I would never care for any girl as I cared for you; and the sooner he realised that the better.

MONICA *(disappointed)* But you've said all that before.

CYRIL Yes, I know, but it was different tonight. I just went for him – I made him listen. I felt I couldn't stand it any longer.

MONICA *(anxiously)* You didn't give in?

CYRIL Give in? *(Offended)* Why do you say that?

MONICA I don't know, but – sometimes I think if you'd stood up to him at the beginning – no, I don't mean that exactly...

CYRIL Stood up to him – that's all very well, but how about money?

MONICA Oh, I know.

CYRIL We can't marry on my pay. Besides – he's been jolly good to me, always. It isn't because he's my father or any rot of that kind – it's simply that he has been jolly good to me.

MONICA *(softening)* I know he has.

CYRIL I don't want to go back on him, that's all. I know he's being as obstinate as a pig about us but that's my fault partly – I've spoilt him. While I was fighting I had to give in to him to sort of comfort the old chap. And the result is he's been a bit out of hand ever since.

MONICA If only he liked me.

CYRIL He does like you. Or he would if he knew you.

MONICA That's it. He won't give me a chance, he won't let me come near him.

CYRIL He'll come round all right – give him time.

MONICA I can make people like me. Now can't I.

CYRIL *(looking at her)* I daresay. In moderation.

MONICA I'm not rotting, Cyril.

CYRIL Nor am I. Who's been liking you lately? Besides me, I mean.

MONICA *(impatiently)* I'm talking about your father.

CYRIL Bar nothing, Monica – do other fellows ever make love to you?

MONICA What does it matter if they do?

CYRIL It matters a lot to me. I hate you going about as you do, with nothing to tell people you belong to me – hate it.

MONICA So do I.

CYRIL You do belong to me, don't you – every scrap of you I mean.

MONICA I suppose so – in moderation.

CYRIL Don't, Monica.

MONICA Don't what?

CYRIL Hold off... I want to kiss you.

MONICA I'm so worried...

The kiss is more serious than either of them expect and leaves them a little shy of each other. They separate – slowly.

CYRIL *(breaking a silence)* Well, as we were saying—

MARY *comes in.*

MARY *(announcing)* Mr Bennet.

MR BENNET *comes in. He has changed very little since he came into this same room ten years ago.*

MONICA *(jumping up)* Oh! Tell Mother, Mary.

CYRIL Hullo.

BENNET *(to* MONICA*)* How do you do?

MONICA *(suddenly becoming an awkward school girl)* How do you do? Mother's in... Won't you sit down?

BENNET Thanks, I've been sitting all day. *(He stands)*

CYRIL He's like a horse. He rests standing, don't you Father?

BENNET I don't know about a horse... *(The conversation drops)* How is Miss Charlotte?

MONICA She isn't very well today, thank you.

BENNET I'm sorry to hear that. *(Pause)* Nothing serious, I hope.

MONICA Oh no, just not very well. *(Pause)*

CYRIL Oh, dash!

LOIS *comes in followed by* BETTY. *She has changed into an evening frock and looks charming. She brings a breath of entire naturalness into the room and* MONICA *brightens with relief.*

LOIS How do you do?

BENNET *(rather stiffly)* How do you do? I'm sorry to disturb you at such a late hour.

LOIS Not in the least – it's the only time I'm at home as a rule.

BENNET I came to see your husband, but I am told he is out.

LOIS In town unfortunately. This child tells me I'm to talk to you instead.

BENNET If you can spare me five minutes.

LOIS *(briskly)* Children, that clock's slow, and plain girls mustn't be late for a dance.

CYRIL Yes, come along. Where's your cloak, Monica?

MONICA In the hall.

PETER *appears at the window – she sees him.*

Oh dash – here's Peter.

CYRIL *(glad to see him)* Hullo, Peter.

MONICA *goes to the window so that she is between him and the room.*

PETER *(looking past her at* LOIS*)* May I come in?

MONICA No, Peter – I mean, not just at the moment. The fact is, you're boosting in where you're not wanted.

PETER Well, that's simple enough, anyway.

LOIS Nonsense, Monica. Of course he can come in.

MONICA Oh, very well!

PETER *come down and shakes hands with* LOIS.

LOIS How are you?

PETER Very fit, thanks... Hullo, Bennet.

They shake hands warmly.

MONICA Goodnight, Mother.

LOIS Goodnight. Don't make a noise when you come home – you'll wake Aunt Charlotte.

There is a chorus of goodnights – they go out.

Now we can talk.

PETER Oh...shall I make myself scarce?

LOIS You don't mind Peter, Mr Bennet?

BENNET *(he looks at her, then shrugs his shoulders)* So far as I am concerned...

LOIS, *sitting down – she is down right sideways to the audience –* PETER *left.* BENNET *centre.*

LOIS It's about those two children, Peter. They want to get married, and Mr Bennet's come to talk it over.

During the following, it must be understood there is no real animus, no tone of scoring off each other. **MR BENNET** *likes* **LOIS** *and perhaps pities her a little. He knows what she has done and respects her for it.*

BENNET Mrs Gaydon, I hate talking business with a lady.

LOIS Oh, you mustn't feel like that with me. I'm a business woman.

BENNET Then you won't mind my saying bluntly at the beginning, that I don't want this marriage.

LOIS *(sympathetically)* I know you don't. What is your reason – bluntly?

BENNET I have other views for my son.

LOIS You mean, more ambitious ones?

BENNET In a sense, yes.

LOIS Won't you sit down?

He does so.

Have you taken it into account that Cyril is very devoted to Monica?

BENNET Yes. I have also taken it into account that he is a young man and is bound to be devoted to someone.

LOIS You think that if we make ourselves sufficiently disagreeable he'll transfer his affections elsewhere?

BENNET I think unsuitable marriages are sometimes prevented by wise treatment on the part of the parents.

LOIS I'm afraid treatment by parents doesn't go very far nowadays.

BENNET What I mean is that Cyril has been here constantly whenever he has been home on leave, without a word of remonstrance from you.

LOIS I never remonstrate unless I am certain of being listened to.

He moves impatiently.

They wouldn't have listened, so I held my tongue.

BENNET Whatever you did does not seem to have had much effect. *(With a sigh)* Though I'm bound to admit that my line has had none either.

LOIS How about giving in?

BENNET Giving in?

LOIS I mean, gracefully of course. Cutting our losses.

BENNET *(stiffening)* Mrs Gaydon, you have misunderstood me. I object to this marriage, and it shall not take place so long as I can prevent it.

LOIS But how are you going to prevent it?

BENNET I allow Cyril five hundred a year.

LOIS In plain words – if he marries Monica you'll stop his allowance?

BENNET That is my meaning.

LOIS But that won't prevent his marrying her.

BENNET A married officer can't live on his pay as Cyril has been accustomed to live.

LOIS No, but with a few hundreds Monica will have, they might get along all right.

Both men look at her.

BENNET Is this a bluff?

PETER Bennet...

LOIS *makes a movement to stop him.*

LOIS I don't understand you.

BENNET *(looks at* PETER *then turns to her again)* You mean you are going to enable Cyril to marry without my consent.

LOIS I don't want Monica to marry without mine.

BENNET What you honestly believe is that my son is an uncommonly good match for your stepdaughter.

LOIS Certainly I do. I also think that Cyril's lucky to get a girl as pretty and healthy and unspoilt as Monica. Isn't he, Peter?

BENNET *(brusquely)* Where are you going to get the money?

LOIS *(quietly)* You can't expect me to answer that.

BENNET From your husband?

LOIS You are dealing with me, not with Eustace.

BENNET So I was ten years ago – nominally – but you gave your husband power of attorney then, and he had absolute control of your affairs.

LOIS I was very young then.

BENNET You were indeed...so young, that if you remember I urged you by every argument in my power not to act as you did.

LOIS Even to trying to dissuade me from marrying my husband.

BENNET Even to that.

LOIS *(steadily)* I wonder that you care to remind me of that, Mr Bennet. *(She looks at him steadily)*

BENNET I still think my advice was good.

LOIS We will leave that, please.

BENNET We can't leave it. I urged you not to marry Eustace Gaydon then for my own reasons. For exactly the same reasons I now urge my son not to marry Eustace Gaydon's daughter.

PETER *makes a movement to rise.*

LOIS *(quickly)* Very well. The question now is, is your son going to take your advice or not?

BENNET I think the question is whether you are going to take my advice or not.

LOIS What is that?

BENNET *(his steady look on her)* Leave this. Let this marriage go – it's best for you, best for us all, believe me.

LOIS Do you really believe it is in my power to prevent it?

BENNET I think it is in your power to do most things, Mrs Gaydon.

LOIS Not to persuade two young people, passionately in love that that love is going to lead to nothing...especially when they know that we are prepared to make Monica a settlement.

BENNET *(with the same steady look)* Out of the private fortune of which your husband has the management.

LOIS *(trying to speak lightly)* Mr Bennet, you're incurable. If we choose to make our daughter a wedding present, how can it matter to you what part of our joint income pays for it?

There is a pause. Then he moves suddenly and speaks in a different tone.

BENNET We'll make a bargain on it... First, what is your idea of a settlement?

LOIS Ah...figures.

BENNET Roughly.

LOIS With Cyril's pay, I suppose they could manage on another – four hundred a year?

BENNET We'll say – ten thousand pounds.

LOIS Ten thousand... Very well.

BENNET *(grimly)* You'll do that?

LOIS Yes. *(Pause)*

BENNET When you do, if you do – I'll agree to withdraw my objection to the marriage.

LOIS And the bargain.

BENNET That's the bargain.

LOIS But I mean to do that in any case, I told you so two minutes ago.

BENNET When you settle this money on your stepdaughter it will be time enough to discuss what I will do for my son.

LOIS I see. I'm to trust you better than you trust me?

BENNET You have my word.

LOIS That's good enough for me, Mr Bennet. *(She gets up)* And now will you forgive me if I leave you? I always go to Miss Gaydon at this time to read her chapter. *(She goes to the bookcase)*

PETER *(filling a silence)* What chapter?

LOIS Oh, the same one – she asks for it every night. *(Takes out a Bible)* "They all shall wax old as doth a garment and like a vesture shalt thou fold them up and they shall be changed". Look – it opens at the place. *(She shows them – holds out her hand)* Goodnight.

BENNET Goodnight.

LOIS Don't go – stay and talk to Peter.

She goes out.

PETER closes the door.

BENNET A very clever woman. But not quite clever enough.

PETER   If I were you I'd feel a bit of a brute.

BENNET   I'm fighting for my son.

PETER   Why can't you go for Gaydon himself instead of bullying her?

BENNET   Because he won't see me.

PETER   That's Gaydon all over. *(Cigar)*

BENNET   Peter – how much does she know?

PETER   How much of what?

BENNET   What we all know. That's he's a rotter and up to his eyes in money difficulties.

PETER   Very little, I should say.

BENNET   Either she's absolutely ignorant, believing what she says, or she knows and is playing his game.

PETER   That's impossible. She's straight, whatever he is.

BENNET   I'm sorry for her if she is.

PETER   Gaydon mayn't be as deep in as we think.

BENNET   Don't tell me. Look at him – look at that Middleton thing. He got out of that by the skin of his teeth. He's been in with one shady lot after another since then. Ask any decent business man who knows him, what he thinks of Gaydon, and he'll tell you to have nothing to do with him... As I told you long ago, only you wouldn't listen to me.

Music.

The band at the Travers' begins to play, heard softly.
He prepares to go.

PETER   I? Oh, my little deal with him doesn't matter much either way.

BENNET   To you, no. But... I sometimes wonder how much it matters to him.

PETER It's a comparatively small thing.

BENNET Is it? It's my belief that Gaydon's affairs are like a house of cards. Pull one out and the whole thing would come down flat.

PETER And bury her in the ruins.

BENNET All right – I'm not suggesting you should do it... *(Moving to the door)* I wonder why this sort of rotter always finds a woman to shelter him.

PETER Why not take a short cut through my place.

BENNET I don't know the way.

PETER *(going to the window)* I'll show you.

BENNET I want a talk with you about your own affairs some time, now you're back.

PETER Any time, if you'll ring me up. The gate's at the end of this path.

They go out by the window, talking.

After a moment the door down right opens and LOIS *comes in, the Bible still in her hand. She follows to the window and listens to the voices, putting the book on a table as she goes, After a moment she comes quickly down.* PETER *comes back.*

LOIS *(nervously)* Hullo, Peter, I thought you'd gone.

He comes down slowly, She crosses to the fireplace avoiding his eyes.

Charlotte's asleep – I shall have to go up again in a minute to see if she's awake. *(Speaking with more manner than is natural)* In the meantime I'll have a cigarette – *(she takes one)* My twentieth today.

He stands watching her as she lights it.

Why don't you tell me I'm smoking too much?

He makes no reply.

(throwing away the match) What have you been doing with yourself all this time?

PETER Waiting for my three months to be up.

LOIS And here you are.

PETER Here I am... Well?

LOIS What did Mr Bennet say about me when I left the room?

PETER What's the matter, Lois?

LOIS Nothing.

PETER You've changed.

LOIS Changed, how?

PETER You used not to humbug.

LOIS I'm not now... Yes, I have changed. I've had time to think. I've stiffened up, Peter – hardened—

PETER Don't, Lois, for God's sake—

LOIS We got wrong before – away from the everyday things. They've come back. All the time you've been away, I've had nothing but that. My work and the house, and Monica and Betty.

PETER And where am I?

LOIS Where you have always been.

PETER Somewhere behind your work and the house and Monica and Betty.

LOIS That's nonsense. I'm simply not going to get you on my nerves again, that's all.

A slight pause.

PETER I've waited three months for this.

LOIS *(almost sharply)* Don't make me pity you.

PETER I don't want your pity.

LOIS Then don't look like that.

He flings away from her towards the window.

Where are you going?

PETER I don't know – anywhere out of this.

LOIS Wait a minute – I... *(He half turns)* I don't mean to be a beast. Honestly.

He turns back into the room with a gesture of half hopefulness.

PETER Oh, my dear.

LOIS *(suddenly her natural self again)* Oh, Peter, let's try and get the best out of this. There's so much I want to tell you, so many things I want to consult you about... Let's just be two friends, glad to meet again.

They look at each other. Then he gives way, goes to her, makes a movement for her to sit down. She does so and he sits beside her.

(In her natural tone) My cigarette's gone out.

PETER You're smoking too much.

She throws it away.

(His elbows on his knees, not looking at her) What about this ten thousand for Monica?

LOIS Ah, that's a bit of a facer, isn't it?

PETER Aren't you rather letting yourself in?

LOIS What else could I do? You heard him.

PETER He thinks he's got you.

LOIS He hasn't.

PETER How do you mean to do it?

LOIS I've made Eustace promise that if I want money for any purpose I think right, he'll let me have it.

PETER And – if he fails you?

LOIS He won't – if he does – I've got a second string to my bow.

PETER What's that?

LOIS A mortgage on the Ginevra's houses.

There is a pause. He looks up.

PETER *(slowly)* And if that fails too?

LOIS Fails? How could it?

PETER *(getting up)* I shouldn't worry, anyway. We'll manage it somehow.

LOIS We...

PETER Why not? What's mine's yours. You know that.

She looks at him.

LOIS Are you offering to lend me money, Peter?

PETER Lend, no—

LOIS Give then – that's worse.

PETER How else are you going to do it.

He is standing in front of her, looking down at her.

LOIS Peter...you don't mean to say that you thought I was relying on you?

PETER What's the use of my having more than my fair share of cash if I can't make Monica happy with some of it?

LOIS Making Monica happy is my job.

PETER So you think. That's where you're making a mistake.

LOIS What do you mean by that?

PETER You've had her all these years, worked and sacrificed yourself for her. Now Cyril's come...and your job is finished.

She looks up at him.

LOIS You mean, that I don't matter any more?

PETER Not quite that.

LOIS Ask Monica if she cares less for me because she's going to be married and see what she says.

PETER She doesn't care less now. But she will. I don't say she'll forget you and all you've done for her. Quite often she'll remember it, and come back and tell you so.

LOIS Come back...

PETER Life has taken hold of Monica. She'll have children – and children make everything else a memory. *(Pause)*

LOIS I've given Monica everything she's ever had.

PETER Look at that poor old woman upstairs.

LOIS Charlotte?

PETER She's been one of the givers too. She didn't marry because an invalid mother wanted her, when all she did could have been done by a paid nurse. She gave up a home of her own to keep house for Eustace when his wife died, you came along and did it better—

LOIS I'm not in the least like Charlotte.

PETER Then don't live like her.

LOIS *(trying to speak lightly)* You're a cheery soul, Peter – aren't you!

PETER It's true, isn't it?

LOIS Oh, that music! *(She gets up with it suddenly on her nerves, goes to the window and shuts it)* Of course you can make life seem frightful, if you stand up above and look down on it. By the time I've finished this little chat with you and read Charlotte's chapter, I shall have had about enough of it.

PETER I've had enough of it the last three months.

LOIS It's no use, Peter, I've told you.

PETER What do you mean me to do?

LOIS I don't know.

PETER Go on – being one of the group – and getting an occasional assurance of your friendship as a reward for my patience! I've loved you for years. And when I couldn't stand it any longer you sent me away for three months – to get over it.

LOIS We couldn't go on as we were.

PETER We are not going on as we are.

LOIS Peter, listen to me... Our love means one of two things. To give it up – or to live as I can't live. Telling lies – hiding things. *(Trying to find her words)...* Monica. Whatever you say, she cares for me. That's all I've had ever since I came into this house. You think of me as separate – I'm not – I'm built into it. You can't take me out.

PETER I don't want to take you out. *(He goes to her)* Lois! They're happy, satisfied; they're fond of you – but they don't suffer for you as I do. How will it hurt them if you come to me—

She makes a movement away from him.

Lois—

LOIS No, Peter!

PETER Who'll be the worse for it if you give me happiness?

LOIS Don't, Peter.

PETER Listen – answer me this! Would Monica give up Cyril for you?

LOIS It isn't the same thing—

PETER You know she wouldn't. You've given them ten years of your life, and because of that you're going to let them dictate how you're going to live another ten years, and another ten after that. I tell you this – they're not going to dictate to me.

LOUIS Peter!

PETER You've got to choose – which is it to be? *(Pause)*

LOIS It isn't fair. I didn't choose when I married – why should I have to chose now?

PETER You've got to.

LOIS *(suddenly)* Sh! *(She listens)*

PETER What is it?

LOIS I heard someone call...

They listen.

PETER I heard nothing...

LOIS There! It was something.

MARY *comes in, pale and frightened.*

MARY Please, will you come...quickly.

LOIS What is it, Mary?

MARY Miss Charlotte – I can't make her hear.

LOIS She's asleep. I went up five minutes ago—

MARY She isn't asleep...her eyes are open. Oh...

She begins to cry – LOIS *hurries out.*

PETER Steady, Mary, She's probably fainted.

MARY Fainted... I think she's – I don't know what to think.

PETER Go to Mrs Gaydon. It's up to you to help her, you know... I'll go and fetch the doctor.

He goes out by the window, the music sounding again as he opens it. **MARY** *pulls herself together and follows* **LOIS**.

The curtain is lowered for a few moments.

Curtain.

Scene II

The same room, two hours later.

LOIS *is sitting in* **CHARLOTTE**'*s chair. She is very still, her face colourless. The lamp beside her is the only light in the room. After a pause* **PETER** *comes in from the garden. They speak in low voices.*

This scene must be played very slowly.

LOIS *(without turning her head)* Is that you, Peter?

PETER I saw the light – I had to come.

LOIS I knew you would. I called you.

PETER Called me?

LOIS In my mind. *(Pause)*

PETER It's one o'clock – why are you sitting up at this time?

LOIS I wanted you. *(Answering him)* Charlotte's dead.

PETER Dead? Poor old woman! *(He comes to her)* Where are they – the others?

LOIS In bed. Asleep.

PETER Has Eustace come back?

LOIS No. I telephoned to his club... I don't know where he is...

He kneels beside her, taking her hands.

PETER Your hands are cold.

LOIS *(shivering)* I'm afraid.

PETER You!

She looks at him.

LOIS Have you ever seen death?

PETER Scores of times, in France.

LOIS I don't mean like that – they were young and people loved them. I mean – *(she makes a movement to the room above)* like this?

PETER No.

LOIS To go out alone, into the dark – with nothing to remember – no one to go to.

PETER You were good to her, you were always good to her.

LOIS I was good to myself, as I shall be.

PETER Don't sit here alone, dear – go to bed and rest.

He is holding her hands, she puts her face down on them.

LOIS Peter, I can't be like her.

PETER Don't think of that now.

LOIS They'll all go away – you told me tonight and it's true – *(she puts her hands on his shoulders, her head bent)* Peter – don't go away... Stay with me...

PETER Lois! *(He lifts her face)*

LOIS Oh, I'm wicked...but I can't live like that...just to be dead at the end of it... I can't...

He takes her in his arms.

Curtain.

ACT II

Scene I

LOIS'*s private room at Ginevra's. Realising the value of the suggestion of prosperity in business, she has given her own personality a suitable setting. However much pinching and planning has gone to make the room, there is no hint of either in the cool-looking linen chair covers which she made herself – the putty-coloured carpet – one of those half-tones that look light, but do not soil easily – and the single red and black lacquer cabinet against the wall at the back.* LOIS *is far too wise to introduce the personal note into business. There are no photographs or mementoes of any kind on tables or mantelpiece, and her writing table might belong to any business man with a taste for good writing things. She herself is wisely dressed in a black charmeuse frock, disfigured for the moment by a pair of white linen half-sleeves, such as are worn by women clerks to keep their cuffs clean. She is writing rapidly.*

MRS GEDDES – *showroom woman to Watteau's during the five years of its life – comes in, carrying a frock over her arm. She is a pleasant-looking Scotchwoman of forty-five or so, trustworthy and serene, with a temperament – or lack of temperament – that enables her to face the endless worries of her job without the smallest waste of nerve tissue. In consequence her face is unlined, her head without a grey hair.*

LOIS *(without looking up)* Is it seven already? *(Sitting left at desk)*

MRS GEDDES A quarter past.

LOIS All right. Just a minute.

> **MRS GEDDES** *turns the frock inside out, shakes it out and lays it on a chair.* **LOIS** *after a moment ceases writing and puts down her pen.*

MRS GEDDES I thought we'd better settle about this. She's sent it back and wants to see you about it at eleven tomorrow.

LOIS *(pulling off her sleeves)* What's the matter with it?

MRS GEDDES She doesn't like the colour.

LOIS *(looking at it)* I don't blame her. Why a woman with mud-coloured hair should want to dress in mud colour, I can't imagine.

MRS GEDDES What are you going to do about it?

LOIS Scrap it and make her another.

MRS GEDDES That's all very well – we did the same thing for Lady Smithers last week.

LOIS It pays in the long run, I'll choose the second frock – and she'll be so pleased with herself in it that she'll never leave me.

MRS GEDDES *(putting down the frock)...* Are you going to catch the early train?

LOIS Not tonight. I want to settle about this advertisement, and if I go home I shan't get a moment's peace. Come here a minute.

MRS GEDDES *(crossing to the table)* I don't know when you do get a moment's peace!

LOIS Oh, in bed. *(Throwing a sheet of paper on the table)* What do you think of that? *(Pause)*

MRS GEDDES A bit plain, isn't it?

LOIS That's the idea.

MRS GEDDES Oh!

LOIS Just the name in good type – *Ginevra. Frocks.* – and the address down in the corner, in case they don't know it already.

MRS GEDDES Nothing about country orders?

LOIS Certainly not.

MRS GEDDES No picture, or anything?

LOIS Oh, Geddes, you're hopeless. I should be a little woman in West Kensington if I listened to you.

MRS GEDDES It's all very well, but who's going to pay for all this?

LOIS The customers. *(She takes a pencil and begins touching up the lettering of the advertisement)*

MRS GEDDES *(drily)* It's lucky there are so many fools in the world, isn't it?

LOIS I don't know about fools. I say, this frock is twenty guineas, take it or leave it. And here I am with more orders than we can carry out.

MRS GEDDES Well, you're safe enough either way. *(Moving away right)*

LOIS Safe?

MRS GEDDES I daresay I should risk a bit too, if I were in your position.

LOIS What do you think my position is?

MRS GEDDES Well – a woman with a husband to back her. *(Opening at back)*

LOIS Yes – of course... I ought to be all right, oughtn't I?

MRS GEDDES *(comes down right centre)* Anyone is in business who can afford to gamble. It's the having to worry about the risk that hampers one...with a smash always hanging over one's head.

LOIS Give me a cigarette, will you?

MRS GEDDES *(offering a cigarette box)* It's empty.

LOIS Oh, good heavens! Where's my case? *(She feels for it in her hand-bag, rather feverishly)* There must be some somewhere.

MRS GEDDES You smoke too much.

LOIS *(irritably)* Oh, nonsense! I work too much and advertise too much, and smoke too much – I'm getting a little tired of hearing about myself. Ah! *(She finds a cigarette, lights it – after a moment's silence)* That rather shows you're right, doesn't it?

MRS GEDDES What does?

LOIS My speaking to you like that.

MRS GEDDES *(serenely)* Well – when a person goes talking away quite pleasant then bites your nose off for no reason, it does show there's something wrong, doesn't it?

LOIS Do I do it often?

MRS GEDDES Pretty often nowadays.

LOIS Nowadays?

MRS GEDDES Well, the last month – since that night poor Miss Charlotte died. That upset you terribly, I know, I could see that, but it is these endless cigarettes as well, whatever you may say.

LOIS I must smoke – it takes the edge off my nerves – stops me thinking.

MRS GEDDES What will Mr Gaydon say about it when he comes home? *(She begins tidying up preparatory to going)*

LOIS Say about – what?

MRS GEDDES Your getting into this state while he's been away.

LOIS *(quickly)* It isn't while he's been away. I was just the same before that night – before Miss Charlotte died – they all noticed it, chaffed me about my temper—

MRS GEDDES Mr Holland thinks you're looking pretty seedy.

LOIS Mr Holland? I haven't seen him for weeks.

MRS GEDDES He's seen you.

LOIS Has he? When?

MRS GEDDES Oh, I don't know – passing in the street, I suppose. Anyway I met him a few days ago and he stopped and asked after you.

LOIS *(lightly)* And I suppose you told him all the nonsense you've been saying to me!

MRS GEDDES Yes, I did.

LOIS And what did he say?

MRS GEDDES Oh, nothing much. Oh, I was to tell you he'd had a good offer for his house and was taking it. I forgot that. *(A silence)*

LOIS I'm – glad he's had a good offer.

MRS GEDDES You'll miss him, being next door all these years.

LOIS Yes.

MRS GEDDES Is there anything else?

    LOIS *looks up at her, slowly.*

LOIS Oh – no, thanks.

MRS GEDDES Then I think I'll be trotting.

LOIS Yes, do. You've had a long day. Goodnight.

    MRS GEDDES *goes to the door and opens it.*

MRS GEDDES Goodnight.

Pause. Door shut.

EUSTACE *is seen on his way in.*

Oh, Mr Gaydon! You did give me a fright!

EUSTACE Good evening, Mrs Geddes.

LOIS *(involuntarily)* Eustace! *(She jumps up and stands staring at him)*

He looks quickly at her, caught by her tone.

EUSTACE Even so... Why this amazement?

LOIS *(trying to speak naturally)* I wasn't expecting you.

EUSTACE You knew I was coming.

LOIS You didn't cable.

EUSTACE *(quietly)* I never do. *(Pause)*

LOIS I was just leaving. I want to catch the early train.

EUSTACE Where's the hurry.

LOIS I've finished here.

EUSTACE I want to have a talk with you.

MRS GEDDES *goes out.*

LOIS *slowly sits down again at her table. She reaches out mechanically for a paper-knife and holds it.*

LOIS What – sort of a time have you had over there?

EUSTACE Bad.

LOIS Hasn't the scheme come off?

EUSTACE No, it hasn't.

LOIS You got my letter about Charlotte?

EUSTACE *(grimly)* I got two letters.

LOIS *(breaking the silence with an effort)* Well, what is it you want to talk to me about?

EUSTACE I want to know what you mean by promising Bennet you'll make a settlement on Monica?

She slowly lets go of the paper-knife. The movement is the only sign of her great relief.

LOIS I'm...sorry you're angry about it – I knew you would be – of course—

EUSTACE Angry! You do this idiotic thing in my absence without consulting me—

LOIS *(quickly)* You left it to me, to act as I thought best.

EUSTACE Did I tell you to promise Bennet ten thousand pounds?

LOIS The night you went away you gave me your word that if ever I wanted money – a big sum, even – you could let me have it.

EUSTACE That's nonsense. You had a headache and were getting jumpy, and I said what I could to cheer you up. *(Move over left)*

LOIS Oh!

EUSTACE If you had told me honestly that you intended to promise Bennet, what do you suppose I should have done?

LOIS You would have refused.

EUSTACE You admit that?

LOIS *(simply)* Yes. That's why I didn't tell you. *(There is almost pleading in her voice)* I had to do it. I had to see Bennet and make some sort of terms with him.

EUSTACE Terms!

LOIS You talked of our needs. This is our need – to get Monica happily married. It's her chance – and – she's going to have it. Somehow. *(Pause)*

EUSTACE *(Holding himself in)* Where do you suppose I am going to find ten thousand pounds?

LOIS I'm not asking you to find it. I want to do it myself.

EUSTACE *(sarcastically)* Out of Ginevra's?

LOIS Out of what your sister left me.

Short pause.

EUSTACE *(sharply)* Don't talk nonsense.

LOIS Eustace – have I ever in my life asked you for money for myself?

EUSTACE What has that to do with it? You go making promises, impossible promises in my name—

LOIS Would you have liked me to tell Mr Bennet I was going to do it out of my own money?

EUSTACE *(finally)* You're not going to do it out of your own money.

LOIS I've given him my word

EUSTACE We'll soon put that right. What's a woman's word in business? *(Sits left)* As for Monica – she must face her disappointment bravely, that's all. After all, she's my daughter and what happens to me, happens to her, in a sense. *(He gets up and stands with his back to the fire)*

LOIS Eustace – have I or have I not the right to do what I like with my own money?

EUSTACE *(frankly)* Of course you have. But this particular thing is out of the question.

LOIS Why?

EUSTACE Because – if you meddle with your capital at this point you'd lose, I won't say half, but a very considerable portion of it.

LOIS I don't propose to meddle with my capital.

EUSTACE What do you propose?

LOIS To transfer the investments to Monica's name. There'd be no loss then.

Slight pause.

EUSTACE *(turns, rises, goes towards her)* And where do I come in?

LOIS You?

EUSTACE *(centre)* I'm your husband, bound to look after your welfare. This idea of yours is a generous one, don't think I don't appreciate that; you're fond of Monica, and like all women where their affections are concerned, you're seeing that and nothing else.

It's my business to see farther – to protect you from a mad impulse of generosity which you would regret as soon as you'd acted on it. If I let you do this, I should always feel that I could have prevented it, and didn't. *(Moves over left)*

LOIS *(her voice hardening)* You can't prevent it—

He looks at her.

Why do you think I did this without telling you first? To force your hand. To make it so awkward for you, that you'd be obliged to give the money at whatever sacrifice.

EUSTACE *(his face hardening)* Then you've failed. *(Moves towards her)* You'll go to Bennet and tell him you've made a mistake and there's an end of it. *(Goes back to table)*

LOIS And leave him to draw his own conclusions. There are rumours already—

EUSTACE *(sharply)* Rumours? What about?

LOIS About you. And Mr Bennet's heard them.

EUSTACE What's he heard?

LOIS I don't know. All I know is that there's something you know and I don't. When I told him we would make a settlement on Monica he didn't believe me.

EUSTACE *(violently)* Then what the devil did you do it for? I told you to keep him hanging on.

LOIS I couldn't do that any longer.

EUSTACE You've promised ten thousand pounds and I haven't ten thousand pence. Nor have you.

LOIS What do you mean?

EUSTACE What I tell you. There's no money. Now you've got it.

A silence.

LOIS Eustace! Where is it? What have you done with it – mine?

EUSTACE How do I know? It's all been together. *(Sharply)* We're married people, aren't we? What's yours is mine?

LOIS It's gone? All of it?... You can't mean that.

EUSTACE I do mean it. *(He meets her eyes and turns away)* Damn it, you've brought it on yourself. If you hadn't done this, you need never have known.

She has risen and stands staring at his back. After a silence he goes on.

I didn't mean to worry you about it. I meant you never to know – I meant to bear it alone...whatever my mistakes have been, you can give me credit for that.

LOIS Mistakes—

EUSTACE *(truculent again)* Well, what else do you suppose, they were?

LOIS *(slowly)* It means that we have nothing in the world, nothing except what I earn?

EUSTACE Well, that's something, isn't it? *(Pause)*

LOIS How did it happen? *(Sits right)*

EUSTACE Oh, I don't know – gradually...in one way and another. *(Irritably)* I tell you I don't know... *(Pause)* Look here – this is a bit of a blow to you, I know that, and... I'm sorry. But it isn't as bad as it sounds. *(His voice begins to resume its ordinary tone)* As I always say, there's a lot to be thankful for. There's always some way of raising the wind for people like us.

LOIS People like us—

EUSTACE *(centre falling back into irritation)* Though how we're going to square Bennet now you've made this ghastly muddle God alone knows. *(Sits left)*

A silence.

LOIS What did you give for these houses?

EUSTACE Seven thousand – why?

LOIS They're worth more than that now.

EUSTACE Of course they are – I did a wise thing to buy them.

LOIS If these houses are worth, say fifty per cent more than they were when we bought them, what would we get for a mortgage on it?

EUSTACE Mortgage? Upon my word, I believe you'd turn me into the street to please Monica.

LOIS Monica is going to be married. Whatever happens to you and me, that's going to be.

EUSTACE I'm not going to talk about mortgages.

LOIS Why not?

EUSTACE I am bound to consider you if you won't consider yourself.

LOIS And if I insist?

EUSTACE You can't. The houses are mine. *(Pause)*

LOIS *(her head bent)* I hate to say it – but do you realise that you are practically dependent on what I earn?

EUSTACE Is that a threat? Or just a pleasant remark?

LOIS It's...a threat.

EUSTACE *(staring – rises; moves towards her)* Upon my soul—!

LOIS *(passionately)* Oh, what is there left for me to do? You stand there like an enemy, fighting everything I do. Even now I don't know if you've told me everything.

EUSTACE Oh!

LOIS Why won't you consider this mortgage?

EUSTACE *(losing his temper)* Because I've taken one out already. And I've a perfect right to do what I like with my own property.

They look at each other. She makes an effort to speak.

LOIS That means... *(Her mind a blank)* What does it mean?

EUSTACE *(beginning to talk himself into the right again)* What's a mortgage? Absolutely nothing, so long as there's no danger of a foreclosure. That isn't going to happen. I give you my word for that.

LOIS Your word...

EUSTACE I know what's in your mind – you're thinking that Ginevra's is affected – jumping to a conclusion as usual. It isn't, it's as sound as it ever was. It's only the idea of the thing. The only difference is that yesterday you didn't know, and today you do. I – I've taken you into my confidence, that's the long and short of it. And it's up to you not to make me regret I've done so.

LOIS *(her voice dead)* What do you expect me to do?

EUSTACE *(cheerfully)* What you've always done – go on working the business.

LOIS Go on – just as long as you pay the interest. Just till one day you will tell me the game's up – and we go down together.

EUSTACE *(centre)* The business is yours just as it always was.

LOIS That isn't true. I know the law. If you fail to pay, they can take this house and everything in it.

EUSTACE I tell you that won't happen.

LOIS You tell me! Have you paid the interest up to now?

EUSTACE That's my business.

LOIS *(rise)* That means that you haven't. *(Passionately)* My God, the years I've worked. And all the time you've been behind me, cutting the ground from under my feet, making all I've done – nothing. *(Her gust of passion over)* I'm going home.

She moves to get her things. She puts her hat on, her back to him, her movements heavy and lifeless. He stands thinking intently.

Who's got the mortgage.

He hesitates.

Who can turn me into the street?

EUSTACE Peter.

For a moment she goes on with what she is doing. Then she turns.

LOIS *(sharply)* What are you talking about?

EUSTACE *(suddenly cool, now that he has come to a decision)* You asked me the question and I've answered it.

LOIS You mean to tell me that Peter has taken a mortgage on these houses? Without telling me?

EUSTACE Why shouldn't he?

There is a pause, then she laughs.

LOIS My dear Eustace, you must think I'm an idiot – an absolute idiot.

EUSTACE Why do you think he ought to have told you?

LOIS To try and make me believe... *(Passionately)* Peter knows what Ginevra's means to me if you don't. He'd never have gone behind my back.

EUSTACE You can see the deed if you like.

LOIS He couldn't have!

EUSTACE All right. It's in the safe at home. *(He turns suddenly to look at the clock on the mantelpiece – comparing it with his watch)*

She stands staring at him.

LOIS *(with a kind of despair)* You and Peter! You two together against me.

EUSTACE There's no question of anyone being against you. Peter saw the chance of a good investment and he took it. We agreed it was better you should not know.

LOIS *(passionately)* We! It was you. Peter was my friend and you traded on that to get him to do this. I'll never forgive you for this, never, as long as I live.

EUSTACE You're like all women, Lois, you can't keep the personal out of a business arrangement.

LOIS I shall ask Peter, I shall ask him.

EUSTACE I think you won't—

LOIS He'll tell me the truth of it.

EUSTACE I said just now that it was agreed you weren't to be told.

LOIS That's just what I am going to ask him about.

EUSTACE *(sharply)* What are you doing?

LOIS I'm going to ring up and find out if Peter's at his flat. *(Takes off the receiver)*

EUSTACE *(sharply)* Put that down!

LOIS City 268.

He comes to her.

Don't, Eustace—

EUSTACE Put it down. *(He snatches the receiver and puts it back, holding her)*

LOIS How dare you do that? Let go of my arm.

EUSTACE I tell you he isn't to know.

LOIS Let go!

EUSTACE *(furiously)* Don't make me say things I shall be sorry for!

She stops struggling – suddenly afraid. The telephone bell rings once – twice. He lets go of her arm.

I'll tell you what you're going to do... Two things... One is – to keep your mouth shut about this mortgage.

LOIS That's impossible!

EUSTACE The other is – to get the money for Bennet.

LOIS *(not looking at him)* How am I to do that?

EUSTACE That's your business.

LOIS I can't borrow, if that's what you mean, I've nothing to borrow on.

EUSTACE What do other women borrow on? You've got us into this mess – get us out... Damn it, you're safe enough with Peter, you know that.

LOIS Peter—?

EUSTACE I ask no questions and I make no difficulties – I've heard enough about this grand friendship of yours. Use it. *(He moves very suddenly)* We'll leave it at that. *(He takes up his coat)*

LOIS *(sits looking straight in front of her, speaks haltingly)* If you'll wait...just a minute, I'll explain why this is impossible.

EUSTACE I don't want explanations. I want to hear nothing more – till you tell me you've got the money.

LOIS We can't ask him, we're too much in his debt already.

EUSTACE We!

LOIS He's a friend – it wouldn't be playing the game. We must think of some other plan. As you say, there are plenty of ways of raising the wind...for people like us.

EUSTACE Listen to me... Why did Peter take this mortgage? Why's he been content to go all these years without a penny interest?

LOIS Because he saw it was a good thing—

EUSTACE Because, if he wasn't your lover, then, sooner or later he knew he would be.

LOIS Eustace!

EUSTACE I've heard enough about my sins – how about yours? Get the money, do you hear me? Get it, and I'll say no more. If you don't—

LOIS You've heard something, someone's been talking, and you think—

EUSTACE I don't think – I know. I knew the moment I came into this room.

LOIS It isn't true.

EUSTACE Say that to Monica. Tell her it isn't true when she asks you.

LOIS Monica?... What are you going to say to Monica?

EUSTACE That's for you to decide. *(He goes to the door)*

LOIS You can't tell her – you wouldn't do that. Eustace – listen—

EUSTACE Get the money.

LOIS It's all over – I haven't seen him for a month—

He goes out.

(following to the door) Eustace!... Eustace!

Door slam.

The curtain is lowered long enough to admit of a change of scene.

Curtain.

Scene II

A room in PETER's *flat in Albany. An hour later. A bell rings. After a moment a* SERVANT *comes in, followed by* LOIS.

SERVANT I'll tell Mr Holland.

LOIS *(goes straight in. Stands centre)* Just say I should like to see him for a few minutes.

SERVANT Very good 'm. Mr Holland won't keep you a moment – he's just finished dressing.

Goes out.

LOIS *moves over right. She goes across the room with a movement of uncontrollable impatience. She is holding on to the mantelpiece when* PETER *comes quickly in.*

PETER *(enters left)* Lois!

She makes a movement but does not turn. He goes halfway to her.

You've come back... *(He goes to her, tries to turn her round)*

LOIS No, no – it isn't that.

He stops.

PETER *(centre)* What is it, then?

LOIS Eustace has come home...

PETER Well?

LOIS *(trying to find words)* He's terribly angry. He...

PETER Angry – what about?

LOIS He's – he knows about you and me.

A silence. They both stand motionless.

PETER How does he know? How can he know?

LOIS He came into my room at Ginevra's. I wasn't expecting that – he's never done it before – and – I...

PETER You gave it away?

LOIS Yes.

PETER Oh, my dear.

LOIS Oh, don't you see how it was? I'd been dreading it so – that first meeting since. But I thought we'd meet at home, with the children there, as we've always done. Then suddenly when he came in – I went to pieces. *(Turning to him)* Peter – if you're angry with me—

PETER Angry!... My dear... Sit down, and let's talk it out. *(Forcing her gently into a chair)*

LOIS *(sitting)* Oh, Peter – isn't it awful?

PETER *(left of chair)* For you, yes. From my point of view – no.

LOIS How can you say that?

PETER I can't leave you now. *(Over left to centre)* *(He looks at her smiling)* There's something doing, now he knows – we've got to be honest at least—

She shivers.

What happened?

LOIS *(trying to collect her thoughts)* It was – Monica – about her settlement. That's what brought it all up.

PETER What on earth has Monica's settlement to do with this?

LOIS I promised Bennet – I meant to do it out of my own money, but that's gone. Eustace is afraid of him – he knows too much. He says – he says I'm to put things right. To get Monica married without his suspecting that the crash is coming. It's come to that – we're down and out – Peter... *(She tries to go on and can't)*

PETER Well?

LOIS *(not looking at him)* Once you offered to help me and I refused.

PETER I remember.

LOIS I want you to help me now… To lend me the money. *(Pause)*

PETER Did he send you to me?… Did he?

LOIS *(desperately)* Will you lend me the money?

PETER *(gently)* No.

LOIS Of course, you must feel that we're a good deal in your debt already—

PETER We…? What do you mean?

LOIS Four years' interest on the mortgage you hold is more than we're ever likely to pay. *(Pause)*

PETER He's told you that, has he?

LOIS Yes.

PETER I did it for you. You believe that, don't you?

LOIS I don't know what to believe.

PETER Lois!

LOIS I'm sorry, I didn't mean that – it doesn't matter now—

PETER Listen. I knew Eustace, and I knew what sort of a mirage you were going to build your business on. You were in his hands – absolutely. I took you into mine. That was all.

LOIS But – not to tell me, even when we talked about it—

PETER Would you have let me do it if I had told you?

LOIS No.

PETER Exactly. And he'd have got a mortgage from any Tom Dick, or Harry who'd have taken him on. Ginevra's would have gone long ago. As it is – you've had five clear years to make good in.

LOIS *(desperately)* Peter – will you let me have the money?

Pause.

PETER *(in his former tone)* What will happen if I do?

LOIS We can go on with the wedding – Monica will be married.

PETER And you?

LOIS I shall go back, go on doing what I've always done, that's all.

PETER Go back – to work your soul out for him – with this in his hands to drive you with.

LOIS Oh, what does that matter?

PETER *(suddenly)* Lois! You know perfectly well I would do anything in the world for you – but you must see I can't do this.

LOIS *(desperately)* If I don't find the money he's going to tell Monica about you and me.

A silence.

PETER My God, of all the... That finishes it.

She looks at him.

LOIS *(eagerly)* You mean – you will?

PETER Give you money – under a threat from him? I'll be damned if I do—

She drops her face on her hands.

LOIS Oh!

PETER *(coming to her, taking her hands)* Lois, you care for me, don't you?

LOIS *(hardly listening)* Oh, yes, yes—

PETER As you did care? This month hasn't changed you?

LOIS Not now, Peter—

PETER Answer me.

LOIS Of course I care... *(Passionately)* But I wish with all my soul you hadn't come that night! It's put everything wrong, that one thing. What am I doing now? Begging you for money. And I've got to go home and tell him I can't get it, and... Oh, my God her face when she knows!

PETER She loves you. And she likes me.

LOIS She'll despise me. We shall never be the same again, and I care so frightfully – I've always cared, ever since she was a little thing... *(Pause)*

PETER *(decisively)* Where is Eustace?

LOIS I don't know – on his way home, I suppose. Why do you ask?

PETER I'm going to see him.

LOIS *(incredulous)* You're not!

PETER What else do you expect me to do.

LOIS You mustn't, indeed you mustn't. You don't know what he's like – wait, wait, just a few days—

PETER I can't do that. What are you going to do?

LOIS Do?

PETER Tonight. You can't go home.

Ring.

A ring is heard. He stops short. There is a pause.

LOIS *(sharply)* Who's that? Are you expecting someone?

PETER No... It can't be – can it?

LOIS Eustace?... He'd never come to you.

They look at each other.

PETER *(motioning to the room beyond)* Come in here – you can come back presently...

She follows him.

If it is, go out by the other door and... Mrs Geddes will put you up, won't she?

LOIS I don't know.

PETER She must.

LOIS It can't be he – he'd never come—

He shuts the door on her. A moment after the SERVANT *comes in.*

SERVANT Mr Gaydon.

EUSTACE *comes in.* PETER, *braced up for a row, sees him more or less his ordinary self – a trifle more uncertain and jerky than usual behind his air of frankness, but no more. He, too, has had time to think things over, and has prepared his own plan of attack.*

EUSTACE Hulloh, Holland. Busy?

PETER No.

EUSTACE Dining out?

PETER No.

EUSTACE Then you can give me five minutes. *(Short pause)* I'm on my way home, as a matter of fact... You're late.

PETER I've got work to do.

EUSTACE Ah, briefs – lucky fellow to have them... Well – I've come to apologise. *(Pause)*

PETER Apologise?

EUSTACE The truth is I have just had a talk with Lois and I lost my temper. Said things I didn't mean – things I knew weren't true all right, but – I said them. May I take one of your cigarettes?

PETER Do.

EUSTACE Good brand, these – I must get some. Well – *(lighting up)* I want to say just one thing. Of course you know, old man – this friendship between you and Lois— *(Throws the match away, making rather a business of seeing if it's fallen on the hearth-rug)* It's all right of course, but it hasn't always been to easy for me to sort of stand aside and look on at it. And today – well, as I say I lost my temper and said things I didn't mean –

PETER What things?

EUSTACE Oh – rot; the kind of rot one does talk. I'm a quick-tempered man and I was riled at Lois's – well rather high-handed action in another matter – Monica's engagement in point of fact. I shall have to eat some humble pie on that too, I expect.

PETER *makes no reply.*

It's beastly awkward talking about these things, but I just want to say that – I – well, have absolute trust in you and Lois – and in short if she tells you anything of what passed, she's making a mountain out of a molehill.

PETER She has told me. She left a moment before you came in.

EUSTACE Ah! *(He is taken aback for a moment – then recovers himself)* Well? – hasn't she been making a mountain out of a molehill?

PETER She told me what you'd said.

EUSTACE And I've told you I didn't mean what I said.

PETER That's a lie.

EUSTACE Come, come, Holland.

PETER You did mean it. I am her lover.

EUSTACE Good God!

PETER As you know very well.

A silence.

EUSTACE *(acting rather well)* You tell me this to my face...? What do you expect me to do?

PETER To threaten me with exposure as you did her.

EUSTACE I tell you I lost my temper – I didn't mean what I said—

PETER That won't do for me. You knew how things were.

EUSTACE I tell you I didn't know! I knew you were her friend but I have trusted to my wife's affection for me – I have loved and trusted her—

PETER Loved her? When have you loved her?

EUSTACE That's my business.

PETER Do you know what you'd do if you cared for her? Kick me out.

EUSTACE So I will if you're not careful.

PETER Not you. You've thought of that – you've realised what you would lose in losing her. Her work, just what she's worth to you. And you've come to me to apologise – My God!

EUSTACE It doesn't strike you that that was a pretty fine thing to do? A pretty generous thing?

PETER Look here, Gaydon. You're going to face this. You're not going to slide out of things for once in your life.

EUSTACE Upon my soul, to hear you talk... You come into my house, make love to my wife – and when I'm too upset to say what I think of you, you defend yourself with a lot of general accusations that no sensible person would listen to.

PETER I'm not defending myself.

EUSTACE You're trying to insinuate that what's happened is my fault.

PETER I'm doing nothing of the kind. I'm telling you why you're trying to get out of it.

EUSTACE It's you who have to get out of it – you and Lois.

PETER We'll leave her alone, please. I take the blame. Now – what are you going to do?

EUSTACE I'm going to give her a chance of saving herself from dishonour – she's my wife – I can't forget that whatever she's done. And the protection of my house and my name are open to her.

PETER So that she may go on earning your living for you?

EUSTACE Insults won't help you, Peter.

PETER What else has she done all these years? You took her when she was a girl, and set her down to slave for you and your children. That's what you call the protection of your house, and name.

EUSTACE She's my wife!

PETER Oh, you married her all right – she was worth marriage. And that's just the difference between you and any hound who takes a woman and exploits her.

EUSTACE Exploits! Because I'm a bit hard up and my wife turns to and helps me—

PETER That's what you've given her in the past. And that's what you mean her to go on doing in the future.

EUSTACE If you have any decency left in you you'll never see or communicate with my wife again.

PETER And leave her at your mercy?

EUSTACE Give her a chance of retrieving herself, of saving her good name – as I am doing.

PETER Damn you and your good name. I'll tell you what you're going to do. You're going to clear out.

EUSTACE Clear out?

PETER Out of England, if you're wise.

There is a silence.

EUSTACE *(staring at him)* I think you're mad!

PETER Will you promise to leave your wife and give me your word you'll never try to see her or communicate with her again?

EUSTACE To hear you, one would suppose you were in my place and I in yours—

PETER Yes or no!

EUSTACE No.

PETER Very well, I'm going to foreclose on the mortgage I hold.

EUSTACE *(stares at him)* It's a trick, a dirty trick to make me keep my mouth shut. My God, Holland, what do you think of yourself now?

PETER So long as the houses are yours she is in your power. By foreclosing on this mortgage I set her free.

EUSTACE You can't foreclose. You'll give me six months notice and I'll pay up.

PETER I'm not afraid of that.

EUSTACE You think you're going to ruin me.

PETER I'm not thinking about you at all... There are two courses open to you – either you clear out for good and all, or you stay and divorce her. In either case she's no more use to you – get that firmly fixed in your mind. You're not going to get another penny or another day's work out of her.

EUSTACE You tell all this to Monica and see how much she thanks you.

PETER You've frightened Lois with that, but you won't frighten me. Whatever she suffers it will be better for her in the end than going on with her life with you. Now you can go. *(Pause)*

EUSTACE Look here, Holland—

PETER That's enough – I've done.

EUSTACE I'll tell you – here are my cards on the table—

PETER Go, I tell you!

EUSTACE *(stands his ground for a moment, then goes to the door – turning)* Damn it, it's all I've got.

PETER That doesn't concern me.

EUSTACE *(his voice low and urgent)* I can't pay. You know that. If you foreclose, everything else goes with it, I give you my word on that. But there are things you don't know of, things I'm in with and that'll make me rich some day, if I can hold on. We'll talk of this – I'll tell you things worth your while.

PETER Oh!

PETER *goes quickly across to the door down right.*

EUSTACE You can't do it, Peter – it means I'm finished if you do, down and out—

The door closes.

Door slam.

What's to become of my children...? *(He stands staring at the door)*

Curtain.

ACT III

*Same as Prologue and Act I. It is four o'clock on a fine
afternoon. The windows at back are open onto the garden
which is bright with October sunshine. Tea is laid on a
table right near the fireplace.*

LOIS *comes in from the hall, goes to bureau left of the
big window, unlocks a drawer and takes out a bundle
of treasury notes; looks about, hesitating; then comes
down to the writing table left and puts the notes on it,
with a letter-weight on the top. Her face is gentle and
moved as she does so. As she goes back to the bureau to
lock it* **MONICA** *comes in hurriedly down right.*

MONICA Luggage labels. Have you got any?

LOUIS There are some in the right hand drawer.

> **MONICA** *crosses to the writing table, sits and pulls out
> the drawer.*

> *(At the bureau, her back turned)* Have you finished the
> packing?

MONICA Yes, they're bringing his things down. *(Finds the labels
– shuts the drawer)* Shall I – what shall I write on these?
(Pause)

LOIS *(At back of chair)* Better leave them... Father will do that
himself when he comes.

MONICA *(very gently)* Don't you even know where he's going?

> **LOIS** *shakes her head, locks the bureau and moves to
> go. As she does so* **MONICA** *sees the notes.*

Did you know you'd left this money here?

LOIS Yes, that's all right.

MONICA There's nearly a hundred pounds!

LOIS I know, I know, it's some Father is going to take on his journey.

She goes out.

MONICA looks again at the money, makes a little movement of compassion and understands. CYRIL appears at the window. His manner is excited, but cool and deliberate.

MONICA Cyril! I said this evening.

CYRIL *(coming in)* I know you did.

MONICA Father's coming – now, in a few minutes – to say goodbye.

CYRIL I can clear out when we hear the taxi. *(He goes to the sofa motioning her to sit beside him)* Come here, I want to talk to you.

She hesitates a moment, then comes and stands in front of him.

MONICA *(very seriously)* Do you know why I asked you to come?

CYRIL Well, I have a sort of notion.

MONICA To offer to release you from our engagement.

CYRIL Yes – you frightful little fool!

MONICA I'm absolutely serious, Cyril.

CYRIL So am I.

MONICA Do you realise that I haven't a bob in the world?

CYRIL Yes, old thing.

MONICA That my father is going smash? *(With an effort)* Doing a bolt?

CYRIL Yes. Peter told me.

MONICA Well – answer then.

CYRIL I have answered. I've said you're a frightful little fool. And now that you've done the right thing and all that – let's drop it! *(He takes her hands)* It's beastly for you.

MONICA More beastly for you. *(She sits beside him)* And perfectly damnable for Mother.

CYRIL I know – if she were anyone but herself, I'd be frightfully sorry for her.

MONICA I suppose one ought to be sorry for Father.

CYRIL Why? He doesn't know he's made a muck of things. I shouldn't wonder if this – bolting, making a fresh start in a new world and all that, isn't really a sort of adventure to him.

MONICA He must feel rotten.

CYRIL Yes, but who's the man in Dickens who took a tin mug to Australia?

MONICA *(rather impatiently)* I don't know.

CYRIL Mac – something – well, anyway, that's the sort of thing I mean. He'll find his feet all right – be jolly happy, probably.

MONICA I wonder if Mother will!

CYRIL Of course she will. And so will we.

She looks at him.

MONICA You've been rather decent about all this, Cyril.

CYRIL Well, you see – I knew.

MONICA Knew what?

CYRIL That this was the sort of thing that would probably happen...sooner or later.

MONICA You knew – a year ago?

CYRIL Bless you yes... I'm sorry, dear, but most people did.

MONICA Why didn't you tell me?

CYRIL How could I? Besides there was nothing definite to tell. That's the queer thing about your father – there never is anything to get hold of.

MONICA It means more waiting for us.

CYRIL Yes. Two weeks.

MONICA Two weeks?

He takes a paper out of his pocket.

CYRIL Just cast your eye over that, my child.

She looks at it, then looks at him in silence.

Rather a neat idea of mine, I think.

MONICA *(realising)* We can't!

CYRIL Why not?

MONICA How can we?

CYRIL It's quite simple – armed with this, we just walk out and get married.

MONICA You mean, without anyone knowing?

CYRIL The Archbishop of Canterbury knows.

MONICA Oh, stop it, Cyril.

CYRIL Sorry – I'm talking like this so that you mayn't feel the least bit rotten about it. I know it's a big step and all that, but it's only doing what we always meant to do, sooner instead of later.

MONICA *(shaking her head)* Not like this.

CYRIL All you've got to do is to take a casual fortnight off in town – we have to be in the parish or something, so Peter tells me—

MONICA *(quickly)* Peter knows?

CYRIL Oh, rather!

MONICA *(slowly)* Is this Peter's idea?

CYRIL What, us getting married? Good Lord, no. As a matter
of fact, I had a bit of a dust-up with Peter on the subject.

MONICA But he's told you what you're to do.

CYRIL Oh, yes, that's since.

MONICA Then what was the dust-up about?

CYRIL Well – we began talking about us and what on earth
was to be done now – and he said – Peter – that it was a
pity neither of us had the spunk to manage our own affairs.

MONICA I like that!

CYRIL I always thought that a successful barrister was supposed
to be a judge of character – didn't you?

MONICA What did you say to him?

CYRIL Oh, I told him what I was going to do – I'd just thought of
the registrar that minute luckily. He caved in then, of course
– washed his hands of the whole business. *(Thoughtfully)*
He particularly said that – about washing his hands.

MONICA Clever Peter!

CYRIL He did make one sensible suggestion about not telling
Mrs Gaydon.

MONICA Does he really expect me to sneak out and get married
without saying a word to her?

CYRIL Well, there's the guvnor. He'll be pretty sick, of course.
And if he finds out afterwards that Mrs Gaydon knew – he'll
go for her. Think it was a put-up job and all that.

MONICA I see.

CYRIL *(judiciously)* Whereas – if we just blow in and say we're
married, what about it? – and there's no one to blame but
ourselves – well, it's no use poor old Dad barking up the
wrong tree, is it?

MONICA *(thoughtfully)* Married!

CYRIL *(drawing a breath)* Yes, by jove— *(Pause)*

MONICA Where shall we go – after we're married?

CYRIL Well, the Ritz is fairly decent – I thought we could dine somewhere and – go to a theatre.

MONICA And when are we coming back to tell them?

CYRIL Oh – the next morning...probably.

She gets up slowly and moves round the sofa.

Or later, if you like...any old time will do, of course.

A silence falls.

MONICA Cyril. *(Centre front of table)*

CYRIL Yes?

MONICA I've got a perfectly awful feeling here.

CYRIL I know, it's the gastric centre.

MONICA Have you got it?

CYRIL *(cheerfully)* Not a bit. Nobody thinks anything of getting married nowadays. *(He gets up, moves round the other side of the sofa)* Well – that's settled. *(Goes slowly round to her – they meet and embrace in silence)* It is settled? Isn't it?

MONICA Yes. And I'll wear my crêpe-de-chine with the fur... Go now, Cyril.

CYRIL *(happily)* I'll come in this evening.

MONICA All right. But don't stay if Mother doesn't want you.

CYRIL Righto!

They go to the window together. LOIS *comes in hurriedly down right.*

LOIS Father's come.

MONICA is outside the window and doesn't hear.

Monica!

She turns.

Father!

MONICA Oh!

She comes into the room, crosses and goes out hastily by the door down right just as **EUSTACE** *comes in by the other.* **LOIS** *is desperately nervous.* **EUSTACE** *has evidently worked himself into an injured mood – his manner is by turns sulky, resentful and reckless. He looks after* **MONICA** *for a moment, his face lowering.*

EUSTACE *(sharply)* What is she running away for?

LOIS *(right of table)* She'll come back presently.

He looks at her resentfully.

EUSTACE You've had your talk with her, that's plain. *(Cross to left centre)*

LOIS I've said as little as I possibly could.

EUSTACE *(bitterly)* A pretty yarn about my sins, I daresay.

She makes no reply.

Well, this is a nice state of things.

She turns as if to say something, the question that she daren't put. **MARY** *comes in bringing the teapot.*

She goes out.

LOIS Mary thought you would like some tea.

EUSTACE Tea! No!

He throws his things on the table like a spoilt child, and goes and sits in a chair by the empty fireplace – and sits brooding while she pours out a cup. Suddenly he turns and their eyes meet for a moment.

LOIS *(cross behind table to left of chair. Speaking rapidly as if she were trying to get in what she has to say before he speaks)* I told them that you were going away because you thought it best for us all. That we – you and I, had got into a mess about money – I said I was as much to blame as you—

EUSTACE As much as I – I like that!

LOIS I made them believe – that we were in it together. It's the least I can do – when you have been so decent to me.

EUSTACE How do you make that out?

LOIS I'm not telling them.

EUSTACE I didn't say I wasn't going to tell them.

There is a silence. Her whole body stiffens then relaxes.

LOIS If you do, I shall kill myself. If you tell them – it will be just that I can't stand it.

EUSTACE And how about me? What if I say I can't stand it?

LOIS You haven't done what I have.

EUSTACE No, thank God!

LOIS What you've done can be excused. They know about it now, and what have you lost? A little dignity –

EUSTACE I'm losing my home, my reputation. What will people say of me? That I've deserted my wife and family when all the time I could have stayed and divorced you.

LOIS *(her head bent)* Oh!... I told you I would go on as we were.

EUSTACE I know how much that means. You're in this with him.

LOIS That isn't true. I begged him not to foreclose.

EUSTACE And you've been begging him all this week, I suppose.

LOIS I wrote – he didn't answer. And I haven't seen him or heard from him since.

EUSTACE Nor have I, curse him! *(With sudden rage)* That's his game – to lie low till he's got me – do you think I couldn't weather this if I wanted to, with six months clear to do it in?

LOIS Then why don't you stay and meet it? This mortgage can't mean ruin to you, unless there are other things besides?

EUSTACE Other things! I'm going because of you, for your sake.

The unreality of the phrase strikes her and she looks at him without speaking.

That possibility hadn't occurred to you, of course.

LOIS No.

EUSTACE What's left for a man to do when his wife cares for another man? There are two courses open to me, as I see it. To ruin you, or ruin myself. *(Goes on, working himself up)* Which is it to be? That's what I've began asking myself day and night, for the last week. And I've made up my mind at last, thank God. *(Pause)*

LOIS You're going away for my sake?

EUSTACE I'm going to make room for another man in your life. That's the truth of it. And you know best what it costs me to do it.

He turns away on this with a slightly theatrical effect. She speaks again without moving.

LOIS Then you meant not to tell them...all the time.

EUSTACE Is that all you have to say?

LOIS *(passionately)* All this week you knew and you've left me to suffer like this, night after night... *(Hurriedly)* I'm sorry – I didn't mean that... *(Pause)* I'm – very grateful to you.

EUSTACE Don't you realise that I'm taking the whole blame? That I'm making myself the scapegoat for both your sins?

LOIS I'm very grateful to you, Eustace...

EUSTACE You do realise?

LOIS Yes, yes.

EUSTACE Very well, I'll go further. I'll give you your freedom.

LOIS *(staring at him)* My freedom?... How can you do that?

EUSTACE By allowing you to divorce me. *(Pause)*

LOIS Eustace!

EUSTACE Oh you can do it, provided I don't defend myself. It's simple enough. You write a letter asking me to return – I refuse. God knows what the law will make of our married life before it's done with it – but that is the law. *(As she doesn't speak)* Well?

LOIS Why are you doing this?

EUSTACE I've told you – for your sake.

LOIS Do you want your freedom?

EUSTACE I want you to have yours – I don't say that in the years to come it mayn't turn out to be the right thing for me too – but that isn't the point – I want you to see that I'm capable of making a sacrifice. I mayn't have been a model husband in some ways – but I don't want you to think that I haven't thought about your future – provided for it, in a sense. *(As of old he is pleased with this little flourish and utterly unconscious of its grotesqueness)*

LOIS Very well... I said just now that I was grateful.

EUSTACE Are you grateful?

LOIS *(getting up)* Oh, it's horrible that we should be talking like this. After all – we've lived together in the same house for ten years; we ought to have some kindness to remember.

EUSTACE There are ways of showing gratitude. *(Pause)*

LOIS I promise you Betty and Monica shall never know anything I can prevent their knowing.

EUSTACE I wasn't thinking of that.

She looks at him – then it dawns on her what he is making for. She looks involuntarily at the money on the table – turns away with a sort of shame.

LOIS *(moving suddenly)* You'll want to see them, I'll call them. *(At door down right)*

EUSTACE Stop a minute. Dash it, we needn't be so nice about it...we're still husband and wife, aren't we?

LOIS Don't ask me, Eustace, please—

EUSTACE If I am a bit hard up, it isn't the first time I've asked you to lend me a bit—

LOIS I know, I know... But don't *ask* me for it. I'll see you again...before you go... I'll come back.

She goes out right.

He makes a furious movement, taking this for a refusal. After a moment **MONICA** *and* **BETTY** *come in. Their manner to* **EUSTACE** *has suddenly become grown up. A mixture of embarrassment and self-control, extremely irritating to* **EUSTACE**. *He pulls himself together as they come in, but the anger is still in his face, and they see it.*

MONICA *(breaking the silence)* Mother said you wanted to see us.

There is another pause.

EUSTACE She's told you how things are.

MONICA Yes.

EUSTACE *(looking from one to the other)* Well, what have you to say about it?

MONICA *(taken aback at the question)* We're very sorry.

EUSTACE You look it. *(Suddenly)* What has she told you?

MONICA *hesitates and looks involuntarily at* **BETTY**.

You don't answer. You can't – is that it?

MONICA *(hastily)* She told us about money, that things had gone wrong.

EUSTACE Anything else?

MONICA No, Father.

EUSTACE *(in the sarcastic vein)* She didn't mention why I was going away – that's a trifle, of course.

MONICA She said – it would make it easier for us.

EUSTACE And you didn't believe her?

MONICA Don't, please.

EUSTACE It happens to be the truth.

BETTY *(finally)* We know the truth.

EUSTACE You don't. *(His irritation getting the better of him)* If you did, you wouldn't put on these grown-up airs with me. You, a couple of children!

MONICA *(movement towards* **EUSTACE***)* Can't we just say goodbye now?

EUSTACE No, you'll listen to me first. *(He pauses and gathers up something of his dignity)* I'm your father – I've the right to justify myself. Because I've got into a bit of a mess about money you think that's all there is to be said. Some day you'll know more – and you'll perhaps come to see that, whatever my faults were, I was capable of doing a big thing – a fine thing. *(He pauses on this)*

MONICA *(lamely)* Yes, Father.

EUSTACE *(feeling he has failed in his effect)* I've been deceived. I've put my faith in people who weren't worthy of my faith. If they'd stood by me, nothing of all this would have happened. But there's this consolation left me – the knowledge that in making this one supreme sacrifice – I'm wiping out any mistakes I may have made in the past.

BETTY *(resenting this for* LOIS*)* Who else has made mistakes?

EUSTACE I'm not going to mention names.

BETTY Why shouldn't you mention names? We don't know the people you have business with.

EUSTACE Business has nothing to do with what I am referring to.

BETTY *(her voice rising)* Then I don't see the use of hinting.

EUSTACE Don't be impertinent!

MONICA *(quickly)* Betty didn't mean that, Father.

EUSTACE And you're as bad as she is.

MONICA I haven't said a word!

EUSTACE Your manner is insufferable. You two set yourselves up to judge me! If you knew a tenth part of the truth you'd lay the blame where it should lie – on other people's shoulders. *(He has moved to the table and sees money)*

BETTY *(turning)* If you mean Mother—

MONICA Betty – Father said people.

BETTY I don't care what he said, he means her. And it isn't fair! *(To* EUSTACE*)* Mother stood up for you! She's always done it, ever since we were children.

There is a moment's pause. Then EUSTACE, *who has been looking fixedly at the money – turns – catching the sense of the last words.*

EUSTACE Stood up for me – what's she had to stand up for?

BETTY She's taken half the blame and you're trying to make us think it's all her fault.

EUSTACE *(furiously)* Half the blame! Half!

MONICA Oh, don't let us talk like this! Betty—

EUSTACE You stand there like judges. You've heard her story – here's mine. She's been false to me. She loves another man.

(He pulls up, startled at his own words) I'm justified, I tell you—

BETTY Father!

EUSTACE *(his back against the table, his hand fumbling at the notes)* I've stood a good deal – but I won't stand being looked down on by my own children – criticized, judged. I'm justified, I tell you. *(Gets money into his pocket. Comes down stage to right of chair)*

MONICA *(she sees him do it – is at the back of the table – a little behind him)* Father!

EUSTACE *(turning on **MONICA**)* What are you looking at me like that for?

*The door down from the hall opens. **LOIS** comes hurriedly in.*

LOIS Your taxi's here. *(She stops short, looking from one to the other)* They've put your things on.

Silence.

EUSTACE *(moving)* Where's my bag?

Nobody moves.

Damn it, where's my bag? *(He takes it up)*

LOIS You can't go like this.

EUSTACE What's there to wait for.

LOIS *(her eyes on **MONICA**)* I want to speak to you alone.

MONICA *(who has not moved)* I'm not going, Mother.

EUSTACE *(going up towards the door where **LOIS** is still standing)* I've had enough of this – you're all against me – every one of you—

LOIS *(almost in tears)* No, no! Wait...you asked me for something...

EUSTACE *(stopping short)* What? *(Cross to desk)*

LOIS You've forgotten.

She goes quickly to the table, finds that the money is gone. She stands for a moment quite motionless – then the truth breaks on her.

Oh, you've got it – that's all right – I meant it for you. It's quite all right. *(Moves)* I'll see you off!

He goes out – she follows him rather blindly.

MONICA *(her eyes on the table)* Did you see that? Did you see that?

BETTY *(coming down to left of* **MONICA***)* What?

MONICA The money – he took it.

BETTY What money?

MONICA Mother's – she put it on that table to give to him and he took it.

BETTY But she – *(realising, awestruck)* – good Lord! Are you sure?

MONICA I tell you I saw!

BETTY She may have told him to take it.

MONICA Then why did he shuffle it into his pocket...like a thief? That's what people are put in prison for. And that's... Father. *(Pause)*

BETTY Oh! Does she know you *saw*?

MONICA No – thank heaven! *(Change of tone)* Look here, Betty... *(She turns and sees that the door is open – goes up and closes it – she speaks without looking at* **BETTY***)* Betty...did you understand what Father said?

BETTY About – Mother?

MONICA Yes.

BETTY *(suddenly awkward)* I – suppose so... *(Turning away)* We can't talk about it.

MONICA We must. *(Coming to centre)* If we don't we'll only go on thinking about it, letting it grow—

BETTY What's the need, if we don't believe a word of it.

MONICA *is silent.*

Monica, you don't believe it? *(Pause)*

MONICA *(slowly, looking straight in front of her)* If I'd been married to Father...and Cyril had come along and cared for me and helped me, as Peter's done...

BETTY Peter? *(A light breaking on her)...* Did Father mean him?

MONICA What else could he mean?

BETTY *(her face clearing)* But – of course she cares for Peter. We've known that all along—

MONICA *looks at her.*

If it's only Peter...

There is an immense relief in her voice. **MONICA** *stands staring at her. In that moment she becomes about ten years older than* **BETTY**. *When she speaks again, it is as if* **BETTY** *were a child.*

MONICA Of course it's only Peter.

BETTY Then what on earth did Father mean?

MONICA What did you think he meant?

BETTY I don't know. It sounded like— *(Suddenly)* I don't know what you feel talking about Mother like this, but I feel a cad – simply! *(Moves left to front of settee)*

MONICA *(moving across to right)* Betty – do you want to help her through his business?

BETTY Of course I do.

MONICA Then here's the way to do it...never to let her know that I saw Father take the money.

BETTY *(taken aback)* I wasn't thinking about the money—

MONICA *(interrupting)* She's always tried to make us think him – decent. Just realise what it would mean to her – to know that he'd put the lid on all that, all she's worked for ever since we were children.

BETTY Do you suppose it's likely I would talk to her about it?

MONICA No – but she might guess you knew.

BETTY She's not going to guess.

MONICA *(decisively)* We'll make a compact... Let's promise each other never to say a word about the money – *(changing tone)* or what Father said about her – as long as we live.

BETTY *(impressed by her tone)* What – wipe it out?

MONICA Wipe it out.

BETTY *(thinks)* But if it's only Peter—

MONICA Never mind that – the money's what matters.

BETTY Oh, all right.

MONICA *(following her)* Give me your word, Betty.

BETTY *(awkward)* I've said all right... Oh, very well; I give you my word.

MONICA And I give you mine. And now we'll go on as if nothing had happened.

She goes to the bell and rings it.

BETTY What's that for?

MARY *comes in, bringing the teapot.*

MONICA *(still in her tone of command)* Tea, please, Mary.

MARY I was bringing it, Miss Monica. *(She puts it down; turns on her way to the door)* Mr Holland rang up a while ago – I forgot to tell you.

MONICA Oh... Thank you.

MARY *goes out.*

Peter... *(She stands motionless, thinking)*

BETTY I'd better go and tell Mother tea's ready.

She moves to go.

MONICA *(suddenly)* No. Wait.

A pause. She crosses to the writing table and takes off the receiver, sits.

Gerrard 268. Yes, please...

BETTY Whatever—?

MONICA Is that Gerrard 268? Is Mr Holland there? Yes, please... That you, Peter? It's Monica. Hold the line, will you? I said, hold the line.

She puts down the receiver, goes quickly out to the garden path, and calls up to the window above.

Mother! *(No reply)* Mother! *(Pause)* Oh, there you are. Do come down.

She comes back to the telephone, takes up the receiver, and waits. The door opens, and **LOIS** *comes slowly in. The last ten minutes alone in her room have left their mark on her; she has pulled herself together to face the worst, without hope or courage. As she comes in,* **MONICA** *speaks.*

That you, Peter?

LOIS *looks up with a quick movement, listening.*

Yes, I did... Happened? Nothing – what should have happened?... Oh, I see. Yes, he's been here – and gone. No, everything's all right, absolutely all right. *(Deliberately)* He just came to get his things, and to say goodbye. Mother – *(with an effort)* Mother gave him some money, and he just said goodbye... *(Gently)* Tired. No... I won't call her, she's – tired... Of course I'm taking care of her – what do you suppose I'm doing? Idiot. *(Gently again)* Yes, I'll tell her... Yes...yes. Goodbye. *(Puts up the receiver, and turns)*

LOIS *closes the door.*

LOIS Was that Peter?

MONICA Yes, he just wanted to know if he could be of any use about business or anything, and would you ring him up when you felt like it – that was all. Except his love, of course.

LOIS Thank you. *(She comes forward slowly)*

MONICA *pushes an armchair forward to the tea table.*
LOIS *sinks into it with an attitude of absolute relief.*
BETTY *sits at the table, and takes up the teapot.*

BETTY *(briskly)* Tea.

MONICA *(beside LOIS)* Tea.

LOIS Tea.

Curtain.

Lightning Source UK Ltd.
Milton Keynes UK
UKHW020419021222
413182UK00009B/483